No Flowers for Their Graves

A Personal Glimpse into Death Row Life

by Janalee Hoffman

JOY PUBLISHING
P.O. Box 827
San Juan Capistrano, CA 92675

Published by Joy Publishing
P.O. Box 827
San Juan Capistrano, California 92675

All Scriptures (spelling, punctuation, and capitalization) are taken from
the Zondervan New International Version Study Bible, Zondervan Bible
Publishers, Grand Rapids, Michigan, © 1985, unless otherwise noted.

Dr. Lloyd John Ogilvie's quote from *The Beauty of Sharing* is reprinted by
permission from Harvest House Publishers, Eugene, Oregon, © 1981.
"No One Expected Me" from *The Dove Cage*, v.4, issue 3, is reprinted by
permission from Dove Flight Ministry, Novato, California, ©1985.

Printed in the United States of America.
10 9 8 7 6 5 4 3 2 1

ISBN 0-939513-49-8

front and back cover illustration by Ricky Sechrest
typesetting by Diane Fillmore
editing by Gina Renée Gross

I am giving you this book because I care. Please accept this gift as a symbol of friendship.

In Jesus' love

_____

Dedication

Nina Beegle, Susan Titus, and Gina Gross

I dedicate this book to you. Without you, I would never have had the courage to write it. Thank you for taking the pressure off my shoulders, transferring it to yours, and allowing me the freedom to have fun as I put this journey with the Lord on paper.

Acknowledgments and Special Thanks

God has blessed our ministry with many special people in these past eight years. Some have been an integral part of us from the beginning, while others labored for awhile before moving on to new mission fields. Although there are too many to name individually, let me say this, "Thank you for your labors of love, financial assistance, and prayers. Without you, this ministry wouldn't exist. You'll never be forgotten because your names are written on the walls of our hearts."

Special Hugs

As "The Mad Hugger," I feel entitled to give special hugs to:

Gary Hoffman, my husband and partner in crime. You taught me how to believe in myself again and you have given me a second set of footsteps to follow in.

Glen White, for encouraging me to write my first article, but especially for introducing me to Jesus.

Henry Dawson, for making me write those first three letters, when I didn't want to.

Steve Braley, for the many hours you spent teaching me how to use my computer, and for bailing me out when I got in trouble with it.

LaWanda White, my cheerleader, devoted friend, prayer warrior, and much, much more.

Table of Contents

CHAPTER ONE
Satan's Playground

"Say to them, 'As surely as I live, declares the Sovereign Lord, I take no pleasure in the death of the wicked, but rather that they turn from their ways and live.'"

Ezekiel 33:11

Cold puffs of air hovered near our mouths like miniature clouds as we stepped from the car one bleak December morning. The gray stone walls confronting us looked as cheerless as the overcast sky. We stepped through the doors of the control room which was housed under a gun tower. My husband Gary and I were asked to empty everything from our pockets except the twenty dollars in quarters we were each allowed to keep in clear, plastic sandwich bags.

Stepping through the metal detector at the brisk command of the officer on duty, we waited our turn to walk across the courtyard to the century-old building that had not aged gracefully. Upon entry we stepped through another metal detector as we were watched by unseen eyes on the other side of a one-way mirror.

Gary was asked to step into a closet-size room. The door closed. I waited patiently in the hallway until he made his exit; then a woman guard ushered me into the same room. My shoes were removed and thoroughly inspected inside and out. "Place your hands on the wall and spread your feet," she told me, not unkindly. She was just doing her job. This I understood, and I didn't mind.

The officer carefully pat-searched my legs and body and ran her fingers through my hair to make sure I wasn't bringing saw blades, weapons, drugs, or other contraband into the prison. Under normal circumstances I would have been embarrassed, but I was too excited to care. The process of the pat-search was done clinically and professionally. She made every effort to prevent any humiliation.

It was Christmas Eve, 1986. We were the first outside prison ministry in history to gain entrance to Nevada's notorious maximum security prison. We were there to visit sixteen brothers in Christ, each a condemned killer on Nevada's death row.

Our prison ministry began in 1983 at a medium security prison in southern Nevada, called Jean Prison, where we ministered for two years. We were primarily a support team for other ministries at that time. Now, this visit to death row is the fruit which grew from eighteen months of correspondence with these prisoners and sharing Christ's love with them.

We entered a large room through sliding doors made of steel and bulletproof glass. The room was a pale cream color and reminded me of the cafeteria at my senior high school, except the school walls weren't stained with years of smoke. Long tables which touched end-to-end spanned the entire length of the room. Chairs formed long rows on either side. A guard named Mike sat on a platform at the far end of the room, looking down the length of the tables. His handsome features were nullified by the stern look his face wore like a mask.

Janet, the female guard who pat-searched me, sat at a table on the other end. While Mike's expression was uncompromising and made us feel like an inconvenience, Janet's smile radiated through her eyes and made us feel

welcome. Every move and action was monitored, not only
by the guards, but by the cameras that moved overhead.
After assessing the situation, Gary and I turned to each
other. Our eyes caught and held for a moment, Gary
winked at me, and we selected two chairs near Janet.

We heard the reverberation of steel doors closing and
the rattle of chains as our guests were escorted to the
visiting room, to meet us for the first time. Everyone
seemed nervous except Gary and me. The men we were
there to meet were considered so dangerous by the prison
administration that they were isolated from other
murderers—locked in a prison within the prison.

Now as we waited to see our friends-by-mail, we heard
chains drop to the floor. A door was nudged open. There
stood three grinning faces—Henry Dawson, Manuel
Lopez, and Roberto Miranda. "Merry Christmas," we all
sang out in unison as we stepped forward without reserve
to collect long-awaited hugs. We were allowed one hug
each before the guards ushered us to the back side of the
table to sit across from them.

"It's about time you guys got here," Henry called out.
"We've all been up since 6:00 A.M. waiting for you." We
laughed at his teasing comment. He knew the visitor's
gate didn't open until 8:00 A.M. Henry had been on the
row for well over a year, and this was his first trip to the
visiting room.

Even though there was nothing remarkable about the
room, Henry's eyes never stopped moving. He seemed to
want to capture every detail, to savor after the visit, when
he was in the tiny cell he called home once again. At six
feet, two inches, Henry towered over everyone. Henry
was convicted and sentenced to death for beating a
woman to death with a soft drink canister.

Roberto was born and raised in Cuba so everyone
called him Castro. He had come to the United States on
the Marielito Boat Lift. With no family or friends in this

country, he had lived on death row over four years
without receiving a visit. Roberto was convicted of
murdering an illegal Mexican alien during a drug deal that
had gone sour.

Roberto spoke and understood English, but when he
spoke fast he was difficult to understand. He was so
excited to have a visit that we had to ask him to slow
down. He flashed us a big grin.

Manuel was of Mexican descent and acted as an
interpreter when Roberto got stuck on a word he was
trying to pronounce. Although Henry and Roberto were
sociable, Manuel was shy. He didn't contribute much to
the conversation, but seemed to enjoy himself. Although
he pleaded innocent, Manuel was convicted of murdering
his stepdaughter.

Because the warden and all the prison staff were
nervous about our visit, we didn't take a Bible or any
religious material into the prison with us. I had brought
some sheets of Christmas music, but because Gary felt
bringing them into the prison would rock the boat, we left
them in the car. The warden had only allowed us into the
prison under sufferance, because the director of prisons
asked him to let us in.

We celebrated Christ's birthday as any family would,
except, of course, there were no Christmas trees or gifts
exchanged. What was exchanged was the spirit of
Christmas—Christ's unconditional love!

We weren't allowed to exchange gifts, but we were
allowed to spend our quarters in the vending machines at
the rear of the room. It contained burritos, microwave
popcorn, soggy tuna salad sandwiches with limp lettuce,
and other assortments of junk food. Gary said the vending
machine constituted "cruel and unusual punishment"! But
the men didn't seem to mind. It was a change from the
usual meal of rice, beans, potatoes, bread, and what some
of them referred to as "mystery meat."

After three hours, again we heard the clang of the outer door and the sound of chains falling to the floor. We learned from Roberto that everyone was being escorted to the visiting room in handcuffs, body chains, and leg irons. The prison "jewelry," as Gary called it, was removed just before they stepped through the door to the visiting room.

We knew from past conversations that each time a man left his cell, he was subjected to a strip search. It was a humiliating experience for every one of them. All their clothes were removed, and they stood naked outside their cells. The inside of the mouth was inspected. Then they were made to bend over and spread the cheeks of their buttocks for inspection of the anus. It didn't matter if a female guard stood by watching. In their bent position each foot was stretched out while toes were spread for inspection. Their hair and beards were also examined.

This is standard practice in all maximum security prisons. Gary and I knew what humiliation these men had gone through to come for this visit.

From the sounds in the hall, we knew two more men were being readied for their visits, and the time with our dear ones had come to an end. We walked around the table and exchanged good-byes, hugs, and a few tears.

Two grinning faces burst through the door and at once I knew one of them was Cary Williams when I heard, "Merry Christmas, Mama." Cary had been calling me Mama for the past year. With him was Jack Mazzan. We didn't know what crimes these men had been convicted of because we never asked. This is the first rule we learned when ministering to prisoners. If the men choose to discuss their pasts with us, we listen with open hearts.

Jack is one of the finest poets I've ever known. He has the ability to be a published author. Cary's knowledge of the Bible astounds me. He spends hours each day studying God's Word. The Holy Spirit has given him a teaching gift.

We all exchanged hugs, and teasingly Gary asked them if I bruised their ribs. I was dubbed "The Mad Hugger."

We made more trips to the vending machines, and even managed to end up with a bag of popcorn that the microwave oven didn't burn to cinders. We teased each other about stringing it, but of course we weren't allowed needle or thread. Even if we were, there was no tree to drape the strings on. We agreed the first Christmas was spent in poverty, and we were keeping with the tradition Jesus started. For the whole three hours each eye twinkled, and, when not indulged in outright laughter, each mouth was curved in a smile.

Without a doubt, the laughter was a joyful noise in God's ears. We forgot we were in a prison, and so did they. Even the guards smiled. I think they forgot too.

During a lull in the conversation, tears formed in my eyes as I realized that these men were condemned to die. As if reading my thoughts, one of them said, "Jan, it's okay. We kiss the chains we wear, because we wear them for Jesus."

We all joined hands across the table—the shared contact felt like an embrace from God. As our hands clasped together I thought, "This is what amazing grace is all about. These men are so despised by society that they are condemned to die, and yet God's grace is sufficient for them too."

A prisoner from the yard who was doing a life sentence was appointed to take snapshots in the visiting room. We had made prior arrangements with the warden to have pictures taken, and they cost two dollars each. We spent fifty-two dollars on pictures, each one a priceless treasure.

Again we heard the outer doors, and we couldn't believe the time had elapsed. Three more men were escorted in. This time the guards didn't usher out the three men we had just visited with. They were thrilled at that unexpected turn of events! The guards allowed them to stay for the rest of the visit.

Gary and I got up to greet our new guests and I heard, "Hello Mother, Merry Christmas." I knew it was Ricky Sechrest. He always called me either Mother or Mom in his letters and over the phone. Everyone had short, cropped hair, except Ricky who favored his hair long. He is outgoing by nature, but I knew his personality would be stifled by so many people surrounding him at one time. He is more comfortable in a one-on-one situation. He remained quiet for most of the visit, preferring to be an observer. We knew Ricky would rather have visited us privately, but with so many friends to see it wasn't possible.

Ricky had been sentenced to death for the murder of two girls. His crime received much publicity, and as a result, Ricky had problems with some of the other prisoners.

Standing next to him was Jeff Farmer. I instantly recognized Jeff because everyone told me I would be taller than him. Instead, Jeff was about two inches taller than I am. Everyone laughed at that. Jeff claimed to be five feet, six inches. I'm barely five feet, one inch tall. I think Jeff stretched the truth a little! Roberto nicknamed me "Five Nothing" but added with a grin, "Just remember Mi Hermana, the most expensive perfume comes in the littlest bottles!"

Jeff was convicted of stabbing an off-duty cab driver to death in his home. In addition to the death penalty, Jeff was sentenced to four life terms without the possibility of parole, plus 160 years.

The third man was Greg Collier. Greg was a good-looking young man who reminded me of the typical kid next-door. He had clear blue eyes, neatly trimmed blond hair, and a gregarious personality. There would never be a lull in a conversation with Gregory around.

Listening to his cheerful stream of chatter, I found it difficult to believe that Gregory was a manic-depressive and that he often sank into deep bouts of depression. Gregory had been convicted of murdering a convenience store clerk. The incident was captured on the store's camera.

Gregory shared with us that he was working closely with a youth group in southern California and was writing letters to many of the teens who were headed for trouble. His goal was to turn them around before they ended up in prison—or worse yet, on death row.

As a result of Gregory's letters, one young girl who was in a juvenile detention facility turned from drugs and alcohol and gave her heart to the Lord. She finished high school and made the dean's honor roll throughout her years in college. She is now happily married.

Gary and I laughed as the men shared with us how they had prepared during the week for our visit: They washed their clothes in tiny sinks and pressed them between the steel slab that juts from the wall and the mattress that lays on top of it. Cary had tried to give himself a home perm, but his hair began to fall out, so he shaved his head. He was so embarrassed he didn't want to come to the visiting room. Everyone was up at the crack of dawn fighting for the first splash in the showers. Gregory got a pimple on his forehead and thought his life was ruined. Henry and Roberto both shaved their heads so Cary wouldn't feel awkward. Ricky's freshly shampooed hair flowed freely down his back, and he had enough hair for all of them. Jack, a hairdresser by profession, just shook his head and smiled.

Gary and I chuckled as they teased us and each other. Here they were, "society's worst," making every effort to make our visit special and memorable.

The time seemed to vanish. Everyone groaned as the guard called out that visiting hours were over for the day.

The presence of God seemed to fill that room, and no one wanted the moment to end.

As Gary and I waited for the warden to give us a promised tour of the prison, Janet came up to us and said, "In all the time I've spent in this prison as a visiting room officer, I've never seen such happiness on so many faces." With that, Janet handed Gary and I a slip of paper and said, "I wrote this for you."

> *The love you show to those in need*
> *Is a lesson to us all.*
> *For there are those whose hate just grows*
> *And whose hearts are very small.*
>
> *The joy you bring is worth much more*
> *Than money could ever buy;*
> *I truly believe within my heart,*
> *You are blessed by God on high!*
>
> *I wish you both much love and health*
> *And may your problems be few.*
> *The world is now a better place...*
> *Just by knowing you.*

While the poem warmed and blessed our hearts, Janet missed something important. No matter what measure of pleasure we were able to give the prisoners, it couldn't compare to the joy they gave to us. We can't even take credit for the love we gave away that day, because that love was secondhand. It came from Jesus.

"I tried to appropriate paint," the warden said, pointing to the stained cement building with the barred windows, "but the state officials said they want this to look like a prison. The hideous building that spans the length of the dirt yard is called the cell house." Behind us he pointed to a door that appeared to be set in the mouth of a primitive, old cave. "That was 'The Hole,' a sort of dungeon where prisoners were confined as a means of severe punishment."

I looked at our surroundings and realized the horror of living in a place like this. We were surrounded by a fence, crowned with razor wire. From my vantage point I could see four towers manned by guards, stalking the platforms with twelve-gauge shotguns. "The shotguns are used as a warning if a fight breaks out or there is an attempted escape. The guards also have rifles. We shoot to kill when necessary," the warden said.

We entered a small, dark building through double security doors. A sign above the door read CMU, which means Condemned Men's Unit. The first door opened to admit us and closed behind us before the second set opened, allowing us entrance into the bowels of death row.

I literally sucked in my breath as we entered death row. The room reminded me of a large, cement tomb. Gary squeezed my hand to convey to me that he was feeling the same emotions that I was.

These men were buried alive while the state warehoused them for execution. The room was dark with few windows. In the center was what looked like a huge cage, made of steel bars. Inside this cage were cells. The cells were so small they fell below federal standards. They appeared to be no more than four by seven feet—smaller than our bathroom. Rather than remodel them to meet federal requirements, a doorway was punched out between two cells and they became one. On one side was a steel slab with a mattress and pillow, and a combination toilet/sink. The other side contained a small yellow plastic box with a cover which held everything they owned.

There were eight men housed on this tier. Eight faces smiled at us and called out greetings. Only the grace of God could put joy in their hearts in such a place of desolation. We only recognized two men on the main floor tier, but it appeared they all knew who we were. Most of the men we had visited earlier lived on the second level. In the weeks prior to our visit a rash of letters came to us from the men, spilling over with excitement. We were hoping the warden would take us to the upper tier because we knew they had spent the better part of the week cleaning their humble little abodes in anticipation of our tour. Some had even made little paper Christmas decorations to brighten up the place so it wouldn't look so dismal. The warden didn't offer to take us up, and we were afraid to ask. We didn't want to risk spoiling the next day's visit.

It was one thing for the warden to take a tour group through who were afraid of the men and quite another to take someone through who viewed them as family. The men learned to ignore the usual procession of people who filed past and scrutinized their cells. It appeared to cause the warden some discomfort to hear them call out cheerful greetings to us. We recognized that he wasn't being ungracious when he rushed us out, just security-conscious. We were disappointed, and we knew the men would be too. They would spend hours in anticipation before they realized we wouldn't see the fruit of their labor.

I thought, "Lord, I can't imagine anyone spending his life in a place like this—and ending up in hell too! I promise I will spend the rest of my life trying to love them into Your arms."

We were allowed a special visit on Friday because we were seeing so many of the prisoners. Fridays are normally set aside for PC visiting. PC is the term used for prisoners who are held in a protective custody unit. They have gotten themselves in trouble with other prisoners and need to be segregated for safety.

Customarily people who have traveled a long distance to visit death row inmates are allowed a second-day visit behind glass. This is called a non-contact visit. The visitor and the inmate are in two different rooms, separated by bulletproof glass, with phones on either side. However, we were given special permission to use a small attorney room so we could have a contact visit. It was cramped with five of us in there, but no one minded. To us it just seemed cozy.

Our first visit on Christmas Day was with Don. We had asked to visit him alone because he had a difficult time getting along with the others, and no one wanted to share the visit with him. The only side of him we ever saw was the perfect gentleman and the committed Christian. But we never doubted the other side was there. Don loved the Lord and spent much time reading his Bible, but he had a difficult time living a victorious Christian life. His tour of duty in Vietnam took its toll on his already damaged psyche, and, in addition, Don had witnessed the murder of one of his parents when he was only three years old. Don was sentenced to death for murdering a doctor while test driving a car the doctor was trying to sell.

As Don was ushered out, Ewok, KiKi, and Big John were escorted in. Everyone called Thomas "Ewok" because he was short and reminded them of the character in *Star Wars*. He spent most of the visit talking about his little boy and how much he missed him, especially at Christmastime. Our hearts went out to him. Thomas was sentenced to death for the rape and murder of a woman who happened to be home during his burglary attempt.

Danny preferred to be called "KiKi." In Hawaiian it means "beautiful from within." Though he stood six feet tall, he only weighed 135 pounds. KiKi had as sweet and gentle a spirit as anyone I've ever met. Listening to him share from his heart was like listening to a poet's insights, and he radiated the spirit of Christ. Our correspondence with KiKi had been limited because he was new on death row, so we didn't know what to expect when he accepted the visit. He was a delightful surprise, and I made a mental note to write to him more often. KiKi has a nourishing personality that makes one feel glad to be with him.

Big John was exactly as I imagined him, tall and husky with a tall and husky personality to match his physique—a bit bossy, a bit opinionated, a bit arrogant, and a bit overbearing. He knew he was all these things, but he refused to be phony. One thing was certain: He loved the Lord, but he was even opinionated about Him. His personality would turn some people off, but Big John didn't care. He wouldn't let many people into his inner circle anyway! I understood Big John, and I could look past the protective shield he erected around himself like a hedge of prickly thorns. I could see the beauty of the rose garden inside. Big John was convicted of being a hired gunman, hired by a husband to kill his wife.

Our last visit of the day was with Randy Moore, Dale Flanagan and Pete Deutcher. Randy and Dale were just nineteen years old when they were arrested and a year later they were sentenced to death. They were the youngest on Nevada's death row. Pete was the oldest and had been there the longest. Randy and Dale had been admitted Satanists on the streets. Their group was comprised of junior and senior high school kids. They were so deeply involved in satanic activities that they actually summoned up a type of demon they called a "Sucubus" that tried to take over their bodies on more than one occasion. Randy explained that a Sucubus drains a person's emotions and that the person can actually feel it inside his or her body.

Dale got involved with the occult in junior high school because it was a way of getting attention. He was introduced to the occult at the age of seven by a relative. He was approached by this relative again at the age of twelve, at which point he spent considerable time researching the subject. In junior high school he made a commitment to Satan, and in senior high school proclaimed his stand. He said, "Jan you wouldn't believe the number of kids that are involved in the occult."

Randy's reasons for joining the occult in senior high school were quite different. When he was a small child, his mother had taken him to a variety of churches. On several occasions, after the services, Randy questioned the pastor or priest about the sermon material, seeking to understand what he had taught. Three times he was told he was evil to ask such questions and that he would go to hell if he kept it up.

Randy honestly believed God hated him. He figured since he was going to hell anyway, he would make the best deal he could for himself before he got there! Dale and Randy were both saved in the county jail, because someone took the time to tell them that Jesus loves them! Reverend Dean spent many months visiting and loving Dale, and led him to the Lord, while Randy was invited by another prisoner to attend a Bible study. Randy only attended to escape the noise in his unit, but instead learned something he had never known before—Jesus loves him.

They have both made the decision to devote the rest of their lives to leading kids out of the occult and teaching them the dangers involved. Satan came to kill, to steal, and to destroy. Dale's and Randy's lives reflect all three of Satan's objectives. Satan is serious about his mission, but Jesus defeated him at the cross. Although Satan lost the war, he is still winning battles. He is a thief and continues to steal souls. Dale and Randy are classic examples of God's saving grace and Christ's promise to create a new person in each of those He saves. Dale has completed over fifty advanced Bible studies offered by Bible colleges and various ministries.

Pete grinned the whole time we were together. His nickname, "The Silver Fox," fits him because his hair is silver-white. Not much of a talker, Pete was more content to sit back and listen. Because of his Roman Catholic upbringing, Pete is reserved in talking about his love for Christ. However, words were not necessary, because the peace of God was written on his face.

Pete was convicted of murdering a prostitute and has been on Nevada's row longer than anyone else. He has been waiting ten years to be executed, never knowing when someone will unlock his barred door and say, "Come on Pete, time to take a walk!" In every letter he wrote during the year before we were able to make the journey to see these men, Pete asked, "When am I going to get my hug?" Finally, Pete got his hug!

"Jan, do you realize only three of those men would have had a Christmas visit if we hadn't made this trip?" Gary asked as we drove our rental car to Reno to catch our flight back home to Las Vegas. "It's hard to believe six of them have never had a visit," he continued thoughtfully. "Where are their family and friends? Do these parents just throw their children away when they get into trouble?"

"Gary, many of their parents didn't stand by them during the good times and many of them were abused as children," I responded with a heavy heart. "Why should we expect them to be on hand when their children's lives have crumbled?"

These men have been damned by society, and judged unfit and worthless by many people. In many cases, the men's families are persuaded by these same judgments and they come to the same verdict. My joy is in knowing Jesus doesn't judge prisoners with the same measure. He scooped down His hand, reached between the bars, and picked up the broken splinters of their lives. Now He is in the process of fitting those pieces back together again. God's love for His children is steadfast and enduring. He hardly approves of everything His children do, but He stands by them.

Unconditional love should be on the top of every Christian's priority list. People anger, disappoint, and I'm sure at times, frustrate God, but that doesn't disqualify them from His love! No matter what these men have done—they are not disqualified from God's love either. Mankind showed Jesus how to die. If mankind has faith—Jesus will show people how to live.

Jesus said, "For I was hungry and you gave me something to eat, I was thirsty and you gave me something to drink, I was a stranger and you invited me in, I needed clothes and you clothed me, I was sick and you looked after me, I was in prison and you came to visit me... Whatever you did for one of the least of these brothers of mine, you did for me" (Matthew 25:35,36,40). We spent Christmas where Jesus lives!

CHAPTER TWO
Is That You Knocking, Lord?

"Here I am! I stand at the door and knock. If anyone hears my voice and opens the door, I will come in and eat with him, and he with me."

Revelation 3:20

"Henry Dawson Arrested for First Degree Murder!" screamed the headlines in our local newspaper on March 8, 1985. Gary and I were stunned. Henry had worked for Gary for over four years. We hadn't seen him in some time, but we were fond of him and knew him to be a gentle man with a delightful sense of humor.

At this time Gary and I had been involved in prison ministry at a medium security prison south of Las Vegas for two years. We knew something of how Henry Dawson felt. We talked it over and decided to send Henry a card to let him know someone cared. On a pretty "thinking of you" card I wrote, "Henry, we're here and we care. It doesn't matter to us if you are guilty or innocent. We were your friends during the good times, and we're your friends now!"

Henry called us two days later, on the day he received the card. He said, "I've been here three weeks and you are the first people to contact me. Thank you for caring; you'll never know how much that card meant to me. I was so despondent that I tried to commit suicide. Your letter gave me hope."

During the eight months that Henry sat in the Clark County Detention Center, we visited him twice a week—as often as jail rules allowed. Neither Gary nor I am a preacher or a teacher by vocation. Rather, we are nurturers and seed planters. We're two ordinary people who love God and have servant hearts.

Henry had worked for Gary as a salesman when Gary was the manager of a men's clothing store named "Stan's of Las Vegas." They became close friends during those years. At night, when Henry knew I walked alone to the parking ramp behind the store, he would escort me to my car. It was easier for him to slip out of the store for a few moments than it was for Gary. Although Gary was much closer to Henry than I was, I learned to care deeply for him during our visits to the jail. We spent those eight months loving Henry into Jesus' arms. Three weeks before Henry went to trial he gave his life to Christ.

In the eight months he waited to go to trial his attorney only went to see him three times, for a half hour each visit. The attorney ordered an investigator to check out Henry's alibi the afternoon before the trial. He failed to contact any of the witnesses Henry had asked him to locate.

During those long months before trial, Henry steadfastly maintained he was innocent. We would have stood by him either way, but we believed him. The evidence was flimsy. Blond hair "like" the victims was found in the car. Henry had just purchased the car from a blond-haired woman whose son had blond hair, and Henry's girlfriend also had blond hair. No fingerprints were found. Six months after his car was impounded, two drops of blood the size of the head of a pin were found by the passenger's rear wheel well. The same as the victim's—and Henry's—O-positive. But the district attorney claimed Henry had B-type blood. (After the trial, Henry was able to prove from his military records he had O-positive blood. His attorney had never checked.)

Henry and a friend had changed the rear breaks on the car just a few days before his arrest. His attorney never tried to contact the friend who had helped Henry change them to see if he nicked himself.

The DA's case against Henry was thin. During the trial a "jail house snitch" named Mike (an inmate who was housed in the same unit with Henry) testified against him. He claimed Henry had made a complete confession to him. Henry and Mike had never gotten along together. In fact Henry had written two "kites" (inmate memos) to the jail's administrator against Mike. The first was because of racial slurs he had made against Henry, calling him a nigger, and the second was because Mike was constantly walking around the day room with no shoes. In the kite Henry complained that Mike had "stinky feet." Henry sent Gary the copies of the kites he had written. Henry's attorney never submitted the kites to the judge. Henry was convicted of first-degree murder, and the jury sentenced him to death.

Gary and I were still going to Jean Prison as volunteers to help the chaplain in services and special programs. Two weeks after the jury convicted Henry, the chaplain phoned me and asked if I would go to the prison with her. The psychologist at the prison asked her to meet with a new inmate who was deeply troubled. The inmate had only been at the prison a few days. The psychologist told the chaplain that he thought the problem was more in her department than his. The chaplain asked if I would go along and provide some kind of religious service for the others while she counseled this man. There were only a handful of men in attendance for the service that evening. After an hour the chaplain stepped from her office into the chapel and asked us all if we would pray with this man, as he had a special burden.

On the side she said to me, "Prepare yourself, Jan. I can't explain, but ask God for strength." Although I was puzzled, I didn't question the seemingly urgent situation, but followed along with the others.

We all knelt together in a circle, holding hands. I was holding the hand of the man we were praying for. He was trembling and crying so hard I feared he would have a heart attack or go into convulsions. I've never heard anyone cry so hard. His hand trembled with such force it was shaking me.

I prayed, "Lord, this man is broken inside. I don't know what is wrong or where he hurts, but you know exactly where all the pieces fit. Please, Lord, put the pieces back together so he can go on to live a victorious life for you. From the cross, Jesus called you Abba...Daddy! You're not some big unapproachable God none of us can reach. You're our Daddy! I see you sitting in a big, soft easy chair, Lord, waiting for your children to crawl up on your lap. I want to place this brother on your left knee so you can hug him against your heart. No one hugs like you do, Father. Let him feel your comforting arms around him. Let him know You are in complete control. I commit him into your care. In Jesus name I pray. Amen." And so it went around the circle until the man we prayed for began to pray.

He was still sobbing and trembling as he cried out, "Oh God, I know I'm responsible for him getting the death penalty. God I just know he wouldn't have been sentenced to death without my testimony! I know it's my fault, I know I'm responsible. Forgive me Lord. Please have mercy on me!"

I was stunned! I wanted to snatch my hand away as though I was holding a poisonous snake. The prison is a forty-five-minute drive from my house and all the way home I was fuming at God. "How could you make me kneel with that man and pray?" I questioned accusingly. I felt used, and I was mad. Yet in my heart, I begrudgingly knew God had a purpose for my being there.

The next evening when we went to visit Henry, I told him what took place at the prison. He said he wanted to write Mike a letter. Gary and I were both apprehensive about Henry writing to him. "Henry, perhaps you should talk to your attorney first," Gary cautioned.

"After I write the letter, I'll let you read it," Henry said with determination. "If you don't think it's appropriate, I won't send it." In the letter Henry told Mike he had become a Christian and was trusting his fate to the Lord. He told Mike he forgave him and asked his forgiveness for writing the kites on him. Gary and I were astounded by the courage it took Henry to write that letter.

"You know," Henry said, "I figure it this way. It's about faith! Faith that God is in control. Maybe someday Mike will come forward and tell the truth; maybe not. But God is still in control and I'll never let anything shake my faith in Him."

The night the judge formally sentenced Henry to death, Gary and I went to the jail to see him. We said, "Henry, you are going to a place we cannot reach. You are a child of the most high King of Kings. That makes you a prince. Hold up your head and be proud. You are a missionary and your mission field is death row. God's hand will be on you to help and guide you. You're not going there alone. Jesus promised He would never leave us or forsake us, and His last words before He left this earth may have been the greatest promise of all. He said, 'Lo, I am with you always, even unto the end of the world'" (Matthew 28:20).

I was a pew-sitting Christian for the first fourteen years of my walk with Christ—a closet Christian. I knew I was a Christian and God knew I was a Christian, but my life wasn't bearing any fruit. I was like a little sailboat out on the ocean. Without God's breath to fill my sail and propel me, I couldn't go anywhere. God was willing, but He was forced to hold the wind in His fist because of my refusal to hoist up my sail. That is the greatest hold Satan has on the church today: leading Christians to sit in the pews and say, "God, show me Your will for my life." Year after year Christians sit there collecting cobwebs like a bunch of dusty skeletons. God wants Christians to do something—anything!

With eyes that couldn't quite meet mine, Henry commented, "But I am so ordinary. How can God use me as a missionary?"

I laughed and said, "Henry, God must have wanted to use 'ordinary' people because He sure made enough of us. Look at the twelve men Jesus selected to proclaim the Gospel to the whole world—a hated tax collector, a bunch of fishermen, and a rebel zealot. They were hardly the upper crust of the community.

"I believe God gave us two arms so we could hug people with broken hearts. He gave us two hands so we could help people in need. He gave us two feet so we could run errands for people who are shut in or sick. Many people have no one to talk to. I think God gave us two ears so we could have a listening ministry. He gave us two eyes so we could watch for a tear in another person's eye. He gave us a mouth so we could share the Gospel."

Then I told Henry about a friend of mine. One day Molly said to me, "Jan, God gave you such a neat ministry. All I know how to do is bake good chocolate chip cookies!"

I said, "Molly, baking good cookies can be a ministry—unless you eat them all yourself. You bake those cookies and you take them to a shut-in or to a nursing home. You give them away with a pat on the hand or a hug and loving words." Molly now has a "cookie ministry."

I was a pew-sitter—not Henry. From the day he was placed on death row, he started witnessing for Christ. His technique was a little rough around the edges, but considering he was only a six-week-old babe in the Lord, it was effective. He had the main ingredient that God looks for in each of us—a willing heart!

Three weeks after Henry was placed on death row he phoned me and said, "Jan, I need your help. There are three guys here asking questions I can't answer. I just don't know the Bible well enough to answer their questions, and I don't want to give them the wrong answers. Will you write to them for me?"

I didn't want to write those letters. I had been going to Jean Prison three times a week, answering sixty letters a month, and working forty-eight hours a week at our jewelry store. However, I told Henry I would because I didn't know how to tell him no. I looked up and said, "Lord, can't you see I'm a very busy person! I don't need more pen pals. Besides, I don't even know what to say to them." (Then I thought, "Well, maybe Henry will forget to send me the names and I won't have to write those letters.")

Two days later Henry sent me the three names. Robert Farmer, Manuel Lopez, and Carroll Edward Cole became my new pen pals. Before I picked up the pen I bowed my head and prayed, "Lord, allow me to be a vessel for your Holy Spirit to write these letters. I don't know what to say that could possibly make a difference in their lives, but You do."

My first letter was to Manuel Lopez. Henry explained that Manuel was a Christian, but he was mad at God. How could a God who loved him allow him to end up in such a mess? I explained to Manuel that God loved him, and that God didn't create situations so He could punish and torment His children. I told him he was mad at the wrong person. What happened to him was a result of sin in the world. I said, "Manuel, Satan gets us coming and going. First he gets us to sin, then he condemns us for being sinners! And if that isn't bad enough, he talks us into believing it's all God's fault!"

I went on to say, "Would you rather have all the power of heaven behind you or all the power of hell? If you turn your back on God, who do you have left to turn to? You have the devil, and he hates you for being God's favorite creation!"

I sent Bibles, Bible studies, and good Christian reading material to Henry and Manuel and encouraged them to hold Bible studies together. I hoped these fledglings could help each other grow.

I learned none of the men had ever seen the chaplain, and they were never allowed to go to the chapel. In fact the prison chapel was turned into a storage area, and the state's only paid chaplain worked in the medium security prison and only went to death row to see a man the day before he was executed. As the only paid chaplain, his energies were split between six prisons which housed over five thousand prisoners.

A Catholic priest who volunteered his time went to see them as often as he was able, but he was too busy to spend quality time with any of them. The men loved Father Dave, but he ministered in three prisons, in addition to running his own parish.

I saw that unless Christians from the outside reached in to those on death row, they would starve spiritually. I began to realize that any Christian can become a missionary from his or her own kitchen table by being a pen-friend, and it isn't necessary to be a Bible authority, just an encourager and a friend in Christ. After all, Gary and I are just two ordinary people trying to follow Jesus' simple definition of ministry: "Love your neighbor as yourself" (Matthew 22:29).

I established a goal to find caring people who would be willing to be a pen-friend to someone on death row who has never experienced God's love and forgiveness, people who have the courage to love someone that no one else wants to love.

Manuel's bitterness diminished as he attended the Bible studies. He still didn't understand why he was being punished, but at least he believed God loved him and was in control. I knew the Holy Spirit would do the rest.

There were days when Henry and Manuel battled with each other. Manuel wanted a day off, and Henry pouted because Manuel wouldn't attend Bible study. "Henry," I counseled, "you can't beat him over the head with the Bible because you will bruise the Word and leave a callous on Manuel's head." Henry still had a difficult time understanding. He thought everyone should instantly fall in love with Jesus as he had. It took him a while to learn that some people have to wait for the Holy Spirit to open some doors for them.

The second letter was to Robert Farmer, and Henry informed me everyone called him Jeff. He told me Jeff doubted God's existence. My first letter to Jeff was like going to the beach. I stick my toes in the water first to see if it is warm or cold. When it is cold, I inch my way in, instead of diving in head first. My first letter to Jeff was carefully constructed so it wouldn't push him away from the message I eventually hoped to share with him. I would be patient and wait for the Holy Spirit to prepare the opportunity.

Jeff kept telling Henry he would write back to Gary and me, but after a month we still hadn't heard from him. Finally he sent us the sweetest letter. He explained that he wasn't a Christian, and that he didn't believe in God. He expressed a desire to be friends, but he let us know he would be uncomfortable talking about God.

We shared letters for months. I'd end my letters with "God bless you" or "I'm praying for you," but I respected his wishes and didn't discuss the Bible or Christ. It was difficult to hold back, because Jeff had all the characteristics that make a Christian shine.

Every Sunday morning at prayer time, I knelt at the altar, and with tears in my eyes asked God to send His Holy Spirit to touch Jeff in a special way. I couldn't write or talk about Jesus, but I prayed he would be able to see Jesus in me.

Once I asked Jeff if I could send him a Bible. I said I didn't care if he read it or not, or if it sat in a corner and collected dust. (I figured if it was there, maybe someday he would be curious enough to open it and read it.) Jeff wrote back and said, "Please don't send me a Bible. My mother sent me one once, and I sent it back. I know it hurt her deeply, and I don't want to hurt you." I never mentioned it again.

Jeff is a fantastic artist. To make a little spending money for shampoo, toothpaste, and other necessities, he makes greeting cards for the other men he lives with. They are so beautiful that even the guards ask him to make cards for them for special occasions. Jeff sometimes sends me a little money to buy him some colored pencils. Once, he called me moments after I received his letter and asked if I had sent the package yet. "Jeff, give me a break," I playfully scolded, "the list just arrived and I haven't had time."

"Be cool, Shorty, I'm not rushing you," he defended with a chuckle. "I know you're busy so take all the time you need. I just wanted to tell you, if you'd like to send a Bible with it, I promise I won't send it back. I won't promise to read it, but I won't send it back."

"Okay," I said without further comment. I wouldn't have embarrassed him for I knew what it cost him to ask for a Bible. The package was express mailed within forty-five minutes!

The substance of our letters gradually changed as Jeff started asking questions. I let him take the lead at his own pace. At first they were "what if" questions.

He'd set up a situation and ask me what I thought. They weren't questions about the Bible, but demanded biblical answers. Even though he disguised his questions, he didn't fool me—and he knew it. Because Jeff had proclaimed for so long and so openly to everyone that he didn't believe in God, he was painfully shy about his new curiosity of Him. I continued to play Jeff's game.

On Good Friday our church held a special service. A huge, crude, wooden cross with splashes of red paint where three spikes had been pulled stood where the altar usually is. All the lights at First Church were off, except the spotlight that illuminated the cross. It had an instantaneous effect on everyone who entered the sanctuary.

As the service progressed we were allowed to go to the cross, pick up a hammer, and nail our worries and cares on the cross, leaving them with Jesus. I walked to the cross and pounded the nail through a little piece of paper that said one word, "Jeff!" With tears in my eyes I looked up and said, "Lord, he's yours! He just doesn't know it yet!"

The next morning Jeff called. After a short conversation I began to sense a change in him. "Jeff, you've been praying haven't you?" I questioned.

"How did you know?" Jeff blurted out, with a mixture of surprise and embarrassment in his voice.

"Jeff," I responded gently, "I'm not sure how I know. I just know! You're different today. I'm going to risk being personal with you even though I promised I'd never push you. When you were praying, did you ask Jesus into your heart?" I inquired.

"No," he stated simply, "I'm not ready for that yet, Jan."

"Jeff," I coaxed, "Jesus has been knocking at the door of your heart for a long time. Isn't it about time you answered it? Jeff, do you believe in God?"

"Yes," he responded with feeling.

"Do you believe Jesus is His Son and that He died for your sins?"

"Yes."

"Jeff, are you a sinner and are you sorry for your sins?"

"I may be the greatest sinner of all and, yes, I'm sorry."

"Then what on earth are you waiting for?" I exclaimed, "Bow your head and let's pray 'Jesus, I love you!'" (There was a pause.) Again I said, "Jesus, I love you." (Again silence.) A third time I continued, "Jesus, I love you."

After a pause I heard Jeff give a tremendous sigh, and even though I was five hundred miles away talking into the phone, I felt those years of resistance melt away. With a choking sound he whispered, "Oh, Jesus I love you!" We continued on with the sinner's prayer.

I told Jeff he had to tell someone that he had just accepted Jesus as Lord of his life. I explained why this was so important and read what the apostle Paul wrote in Romans 10:9, "If you confess with your mouth, Jesus is Lord, and believe in your heart that God raised Him from the dead, you shall be saved." I knew he wasn't yet prepared to tell any of the men he lived with for fear of the ribbing he would certainly receive, but I stressed the importance of telling someone.

The following Sunday was Mother's Day. Jeff's gift to his mother was to tell her she had to share him. He was not only her child, but now he was also a child of God!

My third letter writing assignment was to Carroll Edward Cole. Henry gave me no advice or help at all on this one. I had to write a blind letter, without knowing anything at all about this man. I didn't know whether or not he was a Christian, and I had no idea how old he was.

Again I prayed, "Oh precious Lord, I know there is a purpose for me to write to this man. While I don't know anything about him, You know every beat of his heart and every hair on his head. You know where he hurts. Please put my mind on a single beam with yours, so I'll have the wisdom I need to write this letter. Lord, You give hugs deep inside the heart where they feel the best and mean the most. Help me send Carroll Edward Cole a hug from You!"

That's one letter I'll never lay claim to. The words seemed to fall off the tip of my pen onto the paper. It was my handwriting, but the words belonged to the Holy Spirit. I'd simply been a vessel. I agonized over writing that letter and thought I wouldn't find the words to express. How God must have smiled when I picked up my pen. He already knew what needed to be said; He just needed someone willing to say those words.

Two nights later, as I sat on the floor in front of the television watching the November 1, 1985's top story on the 6:00 P.M. news, the announcer's voice blared, "Death row killer gives up his appeals rights, asks to be executed!" I turned to see if Gary had heard the announcer's opening comments. "It's local and state news," I commented. "It must be someone who lives with Henry. I wonder if they live on the same tier together."

As the news flashed back on, we saw a man dressed in an orange jumpsuit, in handcuffs and body chains. He looked remarkably like Clark Gable. He was standing in a courtroom before a judge. "Carroll Edward Cole," the judge asked, "Do you have anything else to say before I set your execution date?"

"Yes, your honor," he replied, "I understand my rights and I know I can appeal, but I don't want to. I think my crimes deserve the death penalty. Why prolong a despicable person's life who acts as judge, jury, and executioner to people he murdered without regard for the victims?"

The only sound in the hushed courtroom was the hum of the TV cameras as the judge said, "Carroll Edward Cole, I sentence you to die by lethal injection on the morning of December 6, 1985. May God have mercy on your soul!"

I had mailed a letter to this man just hours ago. I knew by the expression on Gary's face he hadn't made the connection. I exclaimed, "Carroll Cole not only lives with Henry, but he is one of the three I wrote to last night."

As I watched this man on TV, the Holy Spirit nudged me to go visit Mr. Cole at the jail, where he would be held until he was returned to death row. I didn't want to go. I did my best over the next two weeks to tune out that small, still voice and pretend it was an overactive imagination. I knew what God wanted me to do, but I was afraid, not that Carroll Cole would hurt me—I already knew from our visits with Henry it would be a non-contact visit behind glass—but for my pride and ego. What if he refused the visit? I'd feel like a fool in front of those guards. He hadn't received the letter I wrote yet, and he didn't know who I was. What if he thought I was some busybody or a reporter looking for a headline story?

The urge persisted, however, until I could no longer ignore it. I said, "All right, Lord, if he is still here, I promise I'll go." Even as I mouthed the words, I harbored the hope that he had already gone.

"Yup, he's still here," the front desk sergeant told me. "But you can't see him until tomorrow night at 9:00 P.M. Be here at 8:00 P.M. so you can sign in for the visit." I didn't have any idea how I was going to break this news to Gary. We had tickets to the UNLV Running Rebels basketball game and we had complementary dinner reservations at a gourmet restaurant where we were meeting friends. The arrangements had been made for weeks. How was I going to explain to him I couldn't go because I had made God a promise? When I explained to Gary what I felt God was urging me to do, he hugged me and simply said, "Honey, you do what you feel God would have you do. I understand."

"He didn't have to be that understanding!" I mumbled to myself. I wanted to go to the game, and I was looking forward to dinner in that fancy restaurant... Compliments of the house, we could have anything we wanted on the menu and it wouldn't cost a dime, except the tip. I didn't need to look at the menu. I wanted steak and lobster! Couldn't Gary see God was sending me to Nineveh just like Jonah? If he had only refused to let me go to the jail, God would have understood and sent someone else.

After Gary left the next evening, I called every friend I knew and tried to talk each one into going with me. "You're going where? Gee, I'd really love to go with you, but I'm terribly busy," seemed to be the standard reply.

As I drove to the jail, I poured out my heart to the Lord. "Jesus, I don't have a clue why you want me to go tonight, but it must be important to you. I have no idea why you chose me. I'll just trust you to give me the words to speak, just as you trust me to go see this man to represent you."

As I stepped up to the desk to sign in for the visit, I was informed someone else had already signed up to see Carroll Cole. The officer on duty was the one Gary and I had gotten to know over the months we visited Henry. He pointed to the man who was waiting to see Carroll and explained if he would give permission to share the visit I could go up with him. If he refused, I would have to wait for another night to visit Mr. Cole because he had signed up first.

Stepping up to this stranger with my most persuasive smile I said, "Hi Mike, I came here to see Carroll Cole. I understand you have already signed up for a visit with him. Would you mind sharing the visit with me? I've driven ten miles to get here." He was very gracious and told me he was there on business, but I could have the first five minutes. I thanked him for his generosity.

As I sat against the wall waiting for the hour to pass so I could go up for the visit, I became woeful. "Well Lord," I said, ticking events off on my fingers, "I missed dinner, good company with old friends, and probably the most exciting basketball game of the whole season, and here I sit in the middle of this seedy jail waiting for a five-minute visit with a man I don't know. Plus I don't even know if he'll agree to talk to me. I don't know what I could say in a half hour that would make a difference, Lord. What can I possibly accomplish in five minutes?"

As we walked into the visiting room, Mike stepped discreetly over by the wall as I took my place at the window waiting for Carroll Cole to come for the visit. I thought I would be nervous, but the words, "My grace is sufficient for you" (2 Corinthians 12:9), kept going through my thoughts. As the guard escorted him through the door, Mike pointed to me and shouted through the glass that I wanted to see him first.

His forehead puckered as he looked at me, as if trying to recall who I was. He took the seat on the other side of the glass and picked up the phone. I smiled and introduced myself. "Carroll," I said, "you don't know me. My name is Jan Hoffman, I'm a friend of Henry's, and I've written to you at his request. He said it was with your permission. When you came down here for court, you missed the letter I sent to you at the prison. I saw you on TV two weeks ago and I decided I'd like to meet you before you were returned to Carson City."

"I'm glad you came," he said, "Henry has talked a lot about you and Gary. It's nice to put a face to your name. Would you please do me a favor and call me Eddie instead of Carroll? All my friends call me Eddie. I've hated the name Carroll all my life."

I nodded my head. "Eddie, I promised your friend Mike I'd only take up five minutes of his visit, so I won't stay much longer. I wanted you to know someone out here loves you. We care that you were born, and we care that you want to die. We're holding out our hands in

friendship. They are safe and warm. I hope you'll reach
for them." He nodded acceptance.

Eddie's eyes never broke contact with mine as I spoke.
I knew by the solemn look in his eyes that he understood
exactly what I was trying to convey. I sensed the Holy
Spirit of God bonding us together, and I felt sure Eddie did
too. I had never felt His presence stronger than at that
moment, and I had never meant words more sincerely than
those I just spoke to this man. Eddie knew it wasn't an
earthy type of love I was talking about, but rather it was
God loving him through me.

As I walked through the sliding security door to leave
the unit, I knew that those were the most important five
minutes in my forty-three years. I didn't know why; I just
knew! I didn't say any of the things I had rehearsed in the
car on the drive to the jail. I didn't even tell him Jesus
loved him. Still I knew I had done what Jesus sent me to
do.

Thanksgiving Day is always special for us. We invite
friends who don't have anyone to share dinner with to our
house. At 5:00 P.M., as the first of our twenty-one guests
arrived for the feast that was ready to be placed on the
tables, the telephone rang. Gary answered it and told me
it was important and I should take the call in the den.

"Collect call from Eddie Cole in Carson City, Nevada.
Will you pay for the call?" the operator asked. I said I
would.

"Hi Jan, Happy Thanksgiving," Eddie greeted
cheerfully. That stunned me for a moment. I didn't know
what to say in return. Here I sat with a house full of
merriment. I was surrounded by family, friends, and loved
ones and a huge twenty-six-pound turkey with all the
trimmings, ready to be served, and this man who lived in a
grim little cell was cheerfully wishing me a happy holiday.

"Eddie," I said, "I hope this isn't an insensitive question.
I want to wish you a happy Thanksgiving, but I don't

want to hurt your feelings. Is it all right to wish you a happy holiday?"

I heard laughter on the other end of the phone. When he caught his breath he said, "Of course it is, Jan, and I appreciate your caring enough about my feelings to ask. It's like this. When you share your happiness out there with us in here we can vicariously celebrate the day through you!"

We teased and talked for a few minutes when Eddie suddenly became serious. "Jan I want to ask you a question." I prompted him to continue because I perceived he was reluctant to ask. "Do you think that God would forgive me for what I've done?"

"Oh Eddie, Jesus already paid the price for your sins when He went to the cross. All you have to do is pray and ask for forgiveness." My heart ached for Eddie. I realized he had carried his sins on his back for years like a huge bag of rocks. He never learned he could leave them at the foot of the cross where Jesus collects all the world's sins. What a trade—sin exchanged for grace! People's sins poured into Christ, and His goodness poured into His children. I tried to convey with my words and the inflection in my voice how much Jesus loved him.

With a note of uncertainty in his voice he continued, "But Jan, I don't know how to pray. Will you pray with me?"

Eddie and I both sobbed as we prayed the sinner's prayer together, a prayer that asks God to forgive one for the sins committed and asks Jesus into the heart. He repeated every word after me and poured out his heart to God. Eddie had belonged to Satan for forty-seven years. Twelve days before his execution Jesus reached down His loving hand and snatched him out of Satan's grasp. I finally realized the importance of my five minute visit to the jail to see him. God wanted Eddie to know how sincere I was, so that my letters would have special meaning when he received them. After reading them, Eddie knew there was someone he could turn to with his broken and contrite heart.

The first letter I received from Eddie was written on November 24, 1985. It arrived the day after Thanksgiving:

Dear Jan and Gary,

You surprised me that Sunday down there in Las Vegas when you came up to see me but I can only chalk it up to God. You see, I was really down, with a lot on my mind and many decisions to make.

I don't know, but you snapped me out of it and I had someone else who cared, and I can't begin to express how that made me feel. I never had too much in the way of friends but then I never let anyone become close, always on guard against hurt.

And I guess you can imagine my reaction with regard to higher matters.

In the last two years my attitude has changed and this is due to serious thinking about myself and others around me. I no longer hate. Quite the contrary.

I wanted to call you the day after your visit, but they couldn't find your name in the directory. I wanted to tell you my feelings, to let you know you lit a light of response. The funniest thing occurred after that visit. A guard at the jail was taking the shackles off me by the sink/fountain in the rotunda and I looked at the shelf. What I seen was a lone Bible and I stood staring and my eyes began to mist. I asked him if I could take the book and he smiled friendly and said I could. He said, "Ed, my wife and I have talked about you and we have some understanding about what happened. I've known you since you came from Texas and although we can never condone what has happened, I myself have seen another side!"

That night I read!

Sure enough your letters awaited me here when I returned to the prison, but I waited until later that night when I was alone to read them. I mean read them! I got a lot from them.

For several months I've had Bibles in my cell that always beckoned (three of them on a stand between book ends, would you believe) to me. I didn't read them because of some stupid idea about running to God when I was in trouble but not when everything was going well.

I think in my own way I was displaying them openly to say where I stood, perhaps to invite discussion (which I never got). To sum up all this rambling, that night you came to offer your friendship, love, and tell me of Jesus' love. You gave me the final push and all this comfort allows me to feel better.

I can snivel, but yet, not snivel, because over all He knows what is in my heart. Oh, I need lots of help but love conquers all. But you're darn right I want your friendship! You got yourself into something now, kiddo. Write soon.

Sincerely,
Eddie

Two days after I received this letter, Henry called and said, "Jan, I'm not really calling for myself. Eddie's execution is getting close and he mentioned that he'd like to visit with you or Gary for a few minutes. It bothers him to phone you because he knows the calls have to be collect. I was sure you'd like to talk to him so I thought I'd call and put him on. Do you mind?"

"Oh Henry, of course not," I responded. "Go tell him I want to talk to him. It will surprise him and he won't feel guilty. Besides, it's the truth, I do want to talk to him."

Within seconds Eddie's winded voice came on the other end of the line. I smiled as I realized he must have ran from his cell to the phone.

"Your letters mean so much to me," Eddie said. "I've read them over and over again. They are comforting and I feel your sincerity. Jan, I want to thank you for praying with me. Since we prayed on the phone, I have felt such peace in my heart. The feeling is indescribable."

"Thank you for sharing that with me, Eddie," I said, "but please don't give me the credit. I helped you with the words, but you are the one who reached out to Jesus and He is the one who took the pain and filled your heart with joy."

"You know, Jan," Eddie said, "it's amazing that a lifetime of reprehensible sins can be wiped off the slate with a simple prayer. Who but God is that loving and forgiving? Lots of people will forgive, but they never forget. God forgives and never remembers the sin again."

On December 4, I received a Christmas card and a second letter from Eddie. Jeff Farmer had made the card for him. The drawing on the front of the card was of a hymn book turned to "Silent Night." In front of it was a lit Christmas candle adorned with holly leaves and berries. The letter said:

December 1, 1985

Dear Jan and Gary,

I'm not much of a letter writer, never was. I just wanted you to know I'm well and that your friendship and love are very much wanted and appreciated.

It's hard for me to put into words my feelings now. Let it suffice to say you came to me when I needed it most. Now I am no longer afraid. Nervous? Yes!

I wanted you to know this so that you'll know there are receptive people in our prisons that not only want, but need, you. If one doesn't, there's another that does, so please don't let selfish, unthinking, and sometimes cruel, people cause you pain. (I know it will anyway but there are always others that need to come to God and His Kingdom.)

If I can get time to myself or can stay awake at night long enough, I'll get off a nice long letter in the next few days. My mind's too muddled right now and I need to get to reading. (The Bible? Yup!)

Every time I start being critical of others I remember Jesus saying, "Why regard the moot in thy brothers eye when there be a beam in thine eye. First remove that which is in your eyes before you consider your brothers," or words to that extent.

Yup, it's hard but when you think in depth and are considerate before you act, the outcome can be quite different. No matter the opinion of some. I love you and thank you for yourselves and for being friends.

Love in Christ,
Eddie

The letter touched me deeply, but I wept as I read what Eddie had written on the Christmas card that accompanied it:

Dear Jan and Gary,

There is no adequate way to express my love for God in words but with acceptance and faith through Jesus Christ. Somehow a great weight has been lifted and I can walk with my head forward and in peace.

Your loving pal in our Lord Jesus,
Eddie

At 2:00 A.M., December 6, 1985 the guards strapped Eddie to the table in the execution chamber and asked him if he was ready. He nodded and smiled. At 2:10 A.M. the warden pronounced him dead. Eddie Cole had murdered thirteen women, but I know when he died Jesus was standing right there with His hand out saying, "Come on, Eddie, let's go home!"

When Eddie was three years old his father was in the service and his mother was having one affair after another. Eddie had one brother and three older sisters who were in school, but his mother dragged him along with her as she met her wooers. Then she would beat Eddie so he wouldn't tell his father. This went on for two years until his father came home from the war to stay. But the beatings continued for years. Her wrath never spilled over onto the other children, but she made up for it on her youngest child.

She dressed him up in girl's clothes and paraded him around in front of her friends. His playmates constantly teased him because of his girlish name, Carroll. He hated the name from a young age.

When he was old enough, Eddie ran away from home and enlisted in the military service. On his first leave from boot camp he decided to go home and visit his family. He stopped in a local bar to have a drink to fortify his courage before he stood face to face with his mother. Sitting at a small table at the back of the tavern, Eddie witnessed his mother sitting at the bar with a strange man. They were fondling each other in plain view of everyone in the bar. It made Eddie so sick that he left the bar and never returned home again.

After that night Eddie's drinking habit increased. If a woman sidled up to him in a bar and indicated she wanted to "party," and especially if she said, "Let's go to your place because my husband is at home," Eddie instantly saw his mother. He murdered his mother over and over again.

He sought the help of many psychiatrists over the years, but they all wanted to place him in group therapy. How could Eddie share his problem in a group?

Until his dying breath Eddie desperately wanted to reach parents who were battering and abusing their children, to tell them of the scars they would leave on these little ones. He wanted to tell them of the ultimate consequences the children might have to pay as a result of their parents' sins. Eddie paid for his mother's sins with his life, although he never used this as an excuse for what he had done. He accepted full responsibility. Some children seemingly survive this kind of abuse and turn out relatively whole. Eddie didn't.

I knew in my heart Eddie wouldn't leave without saying good-bye, but after two weeks of running to the mailbox and returning to the house with a heavy heart, I stopped expecting a letter. On May 8, 1986 Gary went to get the mail and handed me a letter. He said, "Honey, prepare yourself. I hope this isn't some kind of a sick joke." In the top left hand corner was Eddie's familiar handwriting. I didn't understand why it took six months for his letter to be delivered to us, but I knew he wouldn't go home without telling us good-bye. I held the letter for a while without opening it. I wondered if I would cry. I can't express in words my feelings of relief. I knew he had said good-bye!

December 5, 1985

My loving friends Gary and Jan,

I'm real sorry on my letter writing. I'm terrible but I know you know my mental emotions. That Living Bible[1] was just beautiful. Just wonderful and tears came to

---

[1] We had mailed Eddie a Living Bible with a leather cover the day after I met him at the county jail. His name was embossed in gold on the cover. He had expressed that it was difficult for him to understand the King

my eyes when it came to me about 11:00 Tuesday night. Oh sure, 1 had Bibles. Plenty of them! But it was more. Special. And 1'll tell you this. It will be close to me, literally, whatever happens tomorrow morning. This too you can truly believe. 1'm taking it with me!

It's not only that you're a close friend and bring me comfort, as well as joy. 1 believe you are God sent and you're absolutely right, He brought us together. There is no other explanation.

Mike came to visit me yesterday and right after my visit 1 was moved directly to the hold cell (next door to the execution chamber). It came as a complete surprise to almost everyone. And 1 can't have either visits or phone calls, which is sad because 1 so much wanted to talk to you again. 1 would have really liked that. So much went unsaid on my part. My only consolation is 1'll see you again in eternity. That in itself is sufficient. 1 will miss you.

Right now it's 1:00 in the afternoon. 1 have just about all 1 need and 1'm not mistreated. In fact everyone is pretty nice and it's not particularly gloomy...

The guys over at CMU (Condemned Men's Unit) are my friends, and being 1 can't tell them myself, tell them 1 wish them all the best and 1'll never forget them, now or ever. You can tell them 1've accepted Jesus as my Lord and Savior.

You know 1 am a man of few words but had it not been for you as well as Mike and his wife... 1 don't know how 1 could have not crawled the walls.

Sorrow is all right in its own way and it's appreciated because it says a lot. 1 would rather it be not a solemn thing but joyful. 1'm going home!

James Version. It wasn't delivered to him until two days before his execution.

So, loving sister, I'll say bye for now and see you with the Master in Glory. It's been an honor and privilege and wonderful knowing you.

Love,
Eddie

As I handed the letter to Gary to read, I realized I hadn't cried. All trace of sadness was gone. God had given Eddie dying grace. His grace was sufficient for us both.

The day Eddie Cole was executed I was on an emotional seesaw. On one hand I rejoiced because he was in heaven with Christ and that we'd played a small role in giving him happiness in the last few days of his life. But I also mourned because a new friend I'd grown to love dearly through the eyes of Christ was taken from me. It's difficult to let go of someone you hug close to your heart.

I spend a lot of time pouring out my heart to the Lord while I'm in the car. The morning of Eddie's execution, as I was driving to work, my heart was heavy and I cried out, "Lord, are You sure you have the right person for this job? You know how deeply I love people. You also know what a devastating experience it will be for me as these dear ones are executed. I don't think I can handle going through this again!"

God showed me as I prayed that as He gives them dying grace, He will provide me with living grace. He is able to use me because He has given me the ability to unconditionally love the unlovely.

For years I had been so busy being a "Martha, Martha," fretting about the cares of the world, that I forgot to be a "Mary." I learned the importance of taking the time to sit at Jesus' feet and listen to His gentle voice.

Jesus' cares are not of the world—but for the world. He frets for the people who are running in droves straight for the gates of hell! Satan's salesmen are selling lakeshore property in hell, sight unseen, and people are standing in line to buy it. These same people can't believe that Jesus is preparing a mansion for them in heaven—free for the asking. I suddenly realized how close Eddie came to purchasing a plot of land by the lake of fire. What if I had continued to be a Martha? If I hadn't taken the time to be a Mary, would I have missed Jesus' gentle voice? I bowed my head and made Him a promise: "Lord, any door You open, I'll have the courage to walk through!"

CHAPTER THREE
Our Desperadoes

"…Be faithful, even to the point of death, and I will give to you the crown of life!"

Revelation 2:17

After Eddie Cole's execution my husband and I began to realize what a lonely place death row is. The men and women in the mainline prison could go to the prison chapel any time they wanted. They had free access to Bibles, Christian reading material, and for those who couldn't read, the Bible on tape, all provided free by Chaplain Ray Ministries. In addition, various ministries from the free world stood in line trying to get into the minimum and medium security prisons to hold services and Bible studies.

Not so on death row. The prisoners there never saw the chaplain. Gary and I decided to send everyone on Nevada's row a Christmas card with a handwritten note. We wanted them to hear, at least once in their lives, that Jesus loved them. We offered our love and friendship to all thirty-six of Nevada's condemned men and women.

Within a week we heard from twenty-one of them and we were astounded to learn twelve of them were Christians. That is a higher percentage than outside of prison. Almost one-third of the inmates are professing Christians. We continued to correspond and encourage them, and we continued to write to the non-Christians as well. Within a very short time there were six new brothers in the Lord.

The way the CMU was set up, the men were separated on three tiers, eight men to a tier. The CMU holds twenty-four men, and it was full. The overflow was moved to a building called Unit 6. In addition, four men were locked down in the hole, a maximum security unit that is on lock-down twenty-three hours a day.

Henry called Gary and I one Sunday afternoon. During the course of our conversation he explained his living arrangements at the prison. "Our cell doors are opened at 7:30 in the morning and we are locked up again at 9:00 in the evening. The eight men living on each tier are allowed to socialize with each other during this time. Manuel and I are holding Bible studies each day, but I've never seen the other Christian guys you've told me about. They must live on the tier below us. I didn't know there were other Christians here, because we never see each other."

Gary and I learned from Cary, a Christian man who lives on the tier below Henry, that there were three small, fenced-in exercise yards for the men in CMU. When they went to the yard they could mix with those who lived on the other tiers. Eight men were allowed into each yard at one time.

One day when Henry phoned I said, "Henry, you should go out to the yard some day. You've never been out there and that would be a perfect opportunity to meet the Christians from the other tiers. Cary is a fantastic, mature Christian. He could help you understand the Bible better. I know he'd be thrilled to help you with any questions you might have so you don't have to wait for me to answer by mail."

I was puzzled by Henry's response. He was less than enthusiastic over the prospect. In fact, he changed the subject.

"Jan," he said, "one of the guys from this tier is at the jail in Las Vegas for a court hearing. His name is Roberto Miranda. He's from Cuba, but he speaks a little English. He doesn't have anyone in this country except one Catholic nun who writes to him from back East. Would you go see him? I think he could really use a friend."

That night I phoned a friend named Mitch Fox, who is active in ministry at Jean Prison. "Hello Mitch," I said as he answered the phone, "Henry just called from the prison and asked if Gary and I would visit one of his cell mates who is here for a court hearing. He's from Cuba, and as I recall you speak a little Spanish. Any chance of talking you into going along to see him?"

"Sure," Mitch said, "I'll pick you up in an hour."

Only two people were allowed to visit Roberto, so Gary opted to stay home. Having had two heart attacks and open-heart surgery, Gary tires easily.

Roberto was thrilled that someone had come to see him. As there was only one phone on our side of the glass, Mitch and I took turns talking to Roberto. His pronunciation wasn't very good, but his command of the English language wasn't bad if you watched his lips as he spoke.

Mitch started talking about Jesus. He said, "Roberto, do you know Jesus in a personal way? Do you know Him as the Savior of your life?"

With a puzzled look on his face, Roberto asked, "Who is Jesus? I don't know where he lives!"

Mitch turned, smiled at me, and winked. "Many Spanish people name their sons Jesus," Mitch explained to me. He turned back to Roberto and explained in simple terms who Jesus is and what He did for mankind on the cross. He explained all men and women are sinners and need to be forgiven. "Through Jesus every one of our sins could be erased forever from God's memory."

Standing behind Mitch, I nodded my head to affirm everything he said. Roberto looked back and forth at our faces as he absorbed what he heard.

When Mitch finished, Roberto said, "I am from Cuba, I never heard of Jesus or God before. In my country there are things we can't talk about. What must I do to accept Jesus as my Savior?"

Together the three of us placed our hands on the glass window, bowed our heads, and prayed the sinner's prayer.

As Mitch and I left the jail feeling elated, I looked up at him and said, "Well Mitch, that's another one Satan can't have."

Standing in the parking lot before we got into our cars, we prayed, and thanked God for allowing us the privilege of serving Him. We asked Him to strengthen this new brother and to water the seeds we had just planted.

Henry's Bible study group grew by one. When Roberto returned to CMU he became his newest member. Roberto wrote reams of questions for Henry. Henry was growing steadily in his knowledge of Jesus, but had a difficult time keeping up with Roberto's questions. Roberto was hungry to learn, and his keen mind never seemed to slow down.

On one occasion Henry read Romans 3:23, "For all have sinned and fallen short of the glory of God." War was declared! Roberto said, "My mother never sinned!" Henry patiently explained, "We have all sinned except Jesus. That is why Jesus was the 'perfect' sacrifice for our sins, Roberto." Roberto insisted his mother had never sinned.

That prompted a call to us. We confirmed what Henry said and were able to calm him down. "Jannie," Roberto sighed, "you will have to be patient with me. This is all new to me and will take me a while to learn, but I'll try. I love Jesus and I will never lose my faith. I know Jesus loves me too, because I had no one to care for me and Jesus sent you, Gary, and Mitchie to love me. Four years I've been here on death row with no one to care if I live or die except the Catholic nun who writes to me."

Once again I approached Henry about going out to the yard with the other Christian men. "Henry," I said, "you could all have a Bible study together. You could join as one in the Body of Christ and help each other grow."

Finally Henry explained his fear about going out to the yard. He said, "Jan, if a person is going to get hurt here in prison, chances are good it will take place out in the yard. Almost every day we hear the shotguns go off, and we know a guard from the gun tower has shot someone who was in a fight."

"Henry," I said, "trust me. I have been writing to these dear Christian men for months, and you will be so blessed by them. Please try it."

It took a week of planning, but the Christian men of CMU made arrangements with the guards to be placed in the same yard with each other.

I still get tears in my eyes as I recall Henry's phone call following that event. "Jan, it was awesome! We were surrounded by fence and razor wire with a gun tower over our heads. A guard stared down the barrel of a twelve-gauge shotgun the whole time. We started with the only Christian song we all knew, "Amazing Grace." We knew only one verse, so we sang it twice. We followed that with a Bible study. Because we were out for the whole day we were allowed to eat our lunch out there. We wanted to have communion together, but all we had was grape soda and a cookie. We figured if Jesus could turn water into wine, He wouldn't have any trouble with grape soda. Besides, Jesus said, 'Do this in remembrance of Me.' We didn't think it mattered so much to Jesus what we used. The most significant consideration was the motive in our hearts!

"As the day ended, we asked who would like to close in prayer. Jody, who is quiet and hardly ever talks, said he

wanted to be the one to pray. None of us could believe
that Jody had volunteered. Jan, he prayed the most
beautiful prayer. It was a perfect way to end a perfect
day!"

One night as I was answering letters I started thinking
about the emotions those on death row must feel. The
worst part of prison is the loneliness. Mail call is the best
time of day—or the worst! For some, to even receive a
piece of junk mail means "Someone loves me today!" A
prisoner named Jimmy once wrote, "To receive a letter with
a picture is almost as good as a visit!" that.

Gary and I thought our ministry field was Jean Prison.
We had really grown to love the brothers there. As the
months passed our death row ministry required more and
more of our time. We didn't want to leave that prison, but
God slowly closed one door and opened another. Jean
Prison was our boot camp! Without the time we spent
there, we could never have understood what those on the
row were feeling.

As I sat there trying to conjure up a mental picture of
what it would be like to live on death row, experiences
some had shared with me took shape in my mind, and I
penned this poem. It is based on bits and pieces of many
broken lives.

IT'S LONELY LORD

It's lonely Lord in this small dark cell,
my father's gone and my mom's not well.
My wife divorced me yesterday,
how can I kneel... how can I pray?

The friends I ran with on the street,
I thought them cool, I thought them neat!
Not one remembers me today,
they're down the street and on their way.

My dog was taken to the pound,
my kids ask why I'm not around.
How can I tell them I'm in jail,
and the judge has said, "I grant no bail"?

The gavel fell... he caught my eye,
the judge said, "Now son, you must die!"
Yesterday is but a glare,
tomorrow I'll meet the electric chair!

It's lonely, Lord, in this small dark cell,
is this a prelude You call hell?
What's that, Lord... a tear for me?
You gladly died upon that tree?

How can You love me when I'm damned,
can't You see my friends all jammed?
I'm lonesome, Lord, I want to die...
I'm so ashamed but I can't cry.

I've run my life for thirty years,
I've caused more than my share of tears.
I've blown it, Lord, please wash me white,
I give my sins to You tonight.

On bended knee to You I'll pray,
I give my life... now have Your way.
I'll serve You Lord till life is done,
Satan lost and You have won!

"Sparkie" and I will one day meet,
I know I'll have to take that seat.
But You'll be waiting at my side,
all because sweet Jesus died!

I wrote to our new friend Cary Williams for months. Though only twenty-three years old, he was well-grounded in the Word of God and deeply committed in his love for Christ. But one letter he wrote tore at my heart. Cary wrote, "My mother died of cancer when I was only nine years old. She had been sick for two years. Every day I would go into her room, and we would read the Bible together, or just sit and talk. She stressed to me over and over again the importance of an education. She said, 'Cary, you will never make anything of your life unless you have a good education.' She taught me how much Jesus loves us all, and that He should always be number one in my life. One day she called me to her room and had me sit on the bed beside her. She said, 'Cary, I'm going home soon to be with Jesus.' Within hours she died.

"I went to live with my grandmother. She died one year later. After her death I lived with an aunt, but for all practical purposes I was raised by street gangs in Watts. I joined a gang called the Bounty Hunters. By the time I was sixteen I had been shot four times—once in the stomach. They didn't expect me to live. I shot as many people as shot me just trying to survive the madness of the streets. When I was fourteen years old, I stood on the corner talking to a sixteen-year-old friend. A car drove by and the blast of a shot gun tore off his face. What moments before had been my friend was now an unrecognizable mass at my feet. My Vietnam experience took place in the streets of Watts! In spite of my circumstances I continued to attend school and maintain high grades."

I wrote back and said, "Oh Cary, I wish I could have found you when you were that scared, lonely little boy. I would have taken you into my home and raised you like my own baby. You wouldn't always have had steak to eat or expensive clothes. You'd have had lots of hot dogs and hamburgers and some of your clothes would have come from rummage sales, but you would have known incredible love. I know I could never have replaced your dear mother, but I believe I could have earned a place of my own in your heart."

In Cary's next letter he wrote, "I'd be honored to call you Mother." So Mother I became. Cary shared with me his desire to reach kids in street gangs, to help them learn the futility and the dangers, and to show them there is a better way—Jesus! His letter went on to say, "You know, Mama, I would rather be serving Jesus Christ from death row than living on the streets the way I was, because a lot of my friends never lived long enough to make it to death row to find Jesus!"

A man named William Thompson lived on the same tier with Cary. Everyone called William Bud. Bud had been in and out of prison from the age of thirteen when he entered a juvenile detention center. At age forty-nine he had experienced only five years of freedom and had spent thirty-one years of his life in a prison cell. He had no time nor use for "God people" or God. He refused to bend his knee to anyone.

One day when Bud was feeling lonely and blue, he shared his feelings with one of the Christian prisoners. This brother asked Bud, "Do you know that Jesus loves you?" No one had ever asked Bud this before. Bud could not get this thought out of his mind. Because of this simple act of love, Bud knelt by his bed and asked Jesus to be Lord of his life. Cary wrote us and told us that Bud was a new brother in Christ. We sent him a Bible with a black synthetic leather cover. His name was etched in gold letters. Inside the fly leaf I wrote, "Dear Bud, This is more than a book. It's God's love letter to you. Welcome to His family."

Gary and I like to personalize the Bibles we send into the prison. We want the recipient to have pride in holding it in his hand, and we figure if he should get mad at God for some reason, he will be less inclined to throw it away. We received a letter from Bud a week later.

Dear Jan and Gary,

I can't tell you what my new Bible means to me. It is my life and my food! I never read the Bible in my life before, but now I find I can't get enough. You'll never know what it means to me to know that Jesus loves me. I've run my life my way for years. I'm a tired old man, but from now on, I'm going to let Jesus take control of it.

Sincerely,
Bud

One year later Bud gave up his appeals rights and asked to be executed just as Eddie Cole did. Eddie had so much guilt over what he had done that he just didn't want to go on living. He'd let God forgive him, but he never learned to forgive himself. In Bud's case he was a tired old man. He just wanted to go home and be with Jesus. Bud was executed June 19, 1989.

We haven't received his good-bye letter yet. Because Eddie's letter was postmarked exactly six months to the day after he was executed, we believe the prison holds all the inmate's property in a prison property container for six months before it is released. We figured Bud's good-bye letter would be here by Christmas, 1989.

Gary and I have found that each person in prison has his or her own way of doing time. Some who are lucky enough to have a TV watch it virtually twenty-four hours a day. Others sleep their time away, getting up only to shower and eat. Some play chess or cards, and others work diligently to keep their bodies in good shape. Still others have discovered they are very creative, like Jeff

Farmer. Some of Jeff's artwork is breathtaking. He's never had an art lesson, but the cards he designs are beautiful enough to sell in stationery stores. Others are artistic and imaginative in other ways.

Rod Emil does soap carvings using only a paper clip for a tool. He carves swinging hearts on stands and, from a large bar of soap, he carves chains, beginning with a heart padlock on one end, and a key on the other. He also carves stained glass windows with butterflies perched in the center. When held to the light the soap appear translucent. People who see them can't believe he uses only a paper clip for a tool. If a person gives him a clear idea of what he or she would like to have him carve, he'll create it. Rod is also learning to make greeting cards.

Occasionally the physical and emotional involvement of the ministry overwhelms me. Once when I had received an angry letter from someone who was piqued at me, I glanced up and said, "Lord You have a lot of keys on that big ring of Yours, couldn't You open a different door for me and let me join Molly in her cookie ministry?" I was serious, and I was ready to throw in the towel and quit. I felt depressed and discouraged, but I asked God to clearly show me His will in this matter.

Within an hour after I prayed that prayer I received a package from Rod. In it was a charm bracelet made of pink soap, and a swinging heart mounted on a stand, also carved from pink soap, that said, "Jan, we thank you." The package also contained a beautiful card Jeff had drawn that said, "Jan, we just want you to know we love and appreciate all you do for us." It was signed by twenty-seven people from Nevada's death row. God used these dear ones to give me just the hug I needed. He had begun to answer my prayer before I even asked.

Larry Adams is a very talented man; he is a ship builder. He takes bits of cardboard and paper, molds, shapes, and glues them together with toothpaste and milk, stains the finished product with coffee, and ends up with vessels that look like they were made by an expert or from an expensive craft kit.

Ricky Sechrest drew a scale model of Noah's ark based on the account in Genesis. He wanted to surprise me so he gave the plans to Larry, who made the model and a stand so I could put it on display. That gift was followed by a miniature guitar and a small pink heart which could be worn on a chain. I keep them on display at our store. No one can believe how they were made. If they didn't smell like coffee, I'd have my own doubts!

Then there's Jack Mazzan, who paints pictures...with words! His expressive and colorful letters to us were the first indication of his talent. He gave as much care and thought to each word as he did to each stroke of his pen. Jack's flowing, smooth strokes capture his character. He is meticulous in everything he does. Before prison he was a hairdresser by profession. Judging by his perfectionist nature, I'm sure his appointment book was always full.

Henry recently said to me, "Jan, if I'd had a brother, I couldn't have had a better one than Jack. He helps everyone with legal work, a kind deed, or a listening ear. He gives everyone haircuts and never asks for anything in return. He spends hours typing legal briefs for those who don't have attorneys. He even does typing for people he doesn't care for, because he knows they need someone in their corner! Even though he isn't as vocal about his belief in God as some of us are, he shows Christ's love in action!"

Jack is a talented poet. Besides writing hundreds of poems, which he affectionately calls his "children," he has written a full-length novel and a short story. His novel kept me spellbound and I enjoyed his short story, but his strength and proficiency is in his "children"! His collection should be published!

Apparently we are not the only ones who recognized his talent. When Eddie Cole was executed, *The L.V.*

Magazine printed this poem Jack had written for Eddie in their January, 1986 issue.

> *From troubled child to tortured man*
> *A mind that never walked, but ran.*
> *Both hands outstretched in search of hope*
> *For well he knew he could not cope.*
> *That life's design was too oblique*
> *Reality played hide and seek.*
> *Blurred memories of years gone by*
> *Were amplified with liquor's high.*
> *Then rage emerged to take control*
> *With death exacted as the toll.*
> *Repeatedly, the cycle ran*
> *As pain collected in the man.*
> *Unable, then, to stop his ways*
> *With his own life his debt he pays.*

Raised Roman Catholic, Jack is reserved about verbally expressing his affections toward Christ. However, the depth of his feelings flows with grace onto paper. In fact, Jack's sensitivity to people's feelings and his compassion for those who hurt could be a lesson to all.

We have found the men to be marvelously productive, considering their limited resources. God has blessed them with extraordinary talents and they use these talents to glorify the Lord. These men could be totally devoid of joy, but instead, they try to live each day to its fullest, trusting that the Lord is in control. "And they that know thy name will put their trust in thee: for thou Lord, hast not forsaken them that seek thee" (Psalms 9:10).

CHAPTER FOUR
The Rising Son

"You show that you are a letter from Christ, the result of our ministry, written not with ink but with the Spirit of the Living God, not on tablets of stone but on tablets of human hearts."

2 Corinthians 3:3

"Father," I whispered as I knelt beside my bed, "what can Gary and I do to help draw these men together as the Body of Christ so they can encourage each other? We can lead a lost soul home, but we're not Bible scholars. With no one there to guide them, what can we do that would encourage them to bolster each other's faith? It's hard to minister to their needs from five hundred miles away, Father.

"We'll continue writing to them, but they need to learn to be a support team for each other. What would you have us do, Lord?"

As I awoke the next morning, an idea formed crystal clear in my mind. I said, "Gary, I want to print a newsletter strictly for the men and women on death row—a one-time project. If we could get some of the stronger Christians to write a testimony about what Christ is doing in their lives and how He has helped them through the rough times, maybe there are other Christians on the row who will have the courage to stand up and be counted. We both know how difficult it is to be a Christian in prison. Maybe the others will see it's okay to love God! Can we try?"

At that time we were struggling to keep our new jewelry store open at the height of our nation's worst recession. I knew Gary was trying to determine the feasibility of this undertaking before he said yes.

He said, "Jan, if you can get it together, you know I'll back any project you attempt. Money is tight, but we've trusted the Lord in everything else, we'll trust Him in this. If it's His will, He'll make a way."

I wrote to Henry that afternoon and asked him what he thought of the idea and offered some suggestions. I mentioned that I liked what Bylle and Barbara Payton of California were doing in their prison ministry called "Dove Flight." They publish a magazine called *The Dove Cage*, a good, no-nonsense Bible teaching publication for convicts. The articles are written by Bylle, a death row inmate in San Quentin, and put together and distributed by his wife who lives close to the prison. Their magazine's professional appearance and artistic cover immediately catch one's attention.

Henry is on their mailing list, and I knew he would understand what I wanted to do. For the title I suggested *The Rising Son*.

I explained my reasoning for the title: Jesus is the "Risen Son," but you men are each a rising son as the Holy Spirit touches you one by one. If you are interested in this idea, you might check and see if anyone would like to do some artwork for the cover. Maybe a view of the world through a set of prison bars? See if Manuel and Roberto would write an article, and I'll check with the men on the other tiers. I realize it will take a lot of courage to put a testimony in writing. If no one expresses an interest, I will certainly understand, Henry. It's difficult enough for you to carry a Bible under your arm in that place. Putting your thoughts and feelings on paper for everyone on the row to read will be even more challenging."

Henry wrote back, "Jan, the idea is just terrific! Manuel, Roberto, and I will each write an article, and there is a youngster here who also wants to write an article and a poem. Ricky Sechrest does beautiful artwork, and he has even agreed to do the front and back covers. We're all working on it right now. Please drop Ricky a few lines. He's a good kid. You and Gary will like him. Incidentally, we like the name you suggested for the newsletter."

Although I can't draw good stick people, I did a rough sketch of what I thought might make an interesting cover. I wrote to Ricky and received a delightful letter in return. His enthusiasm was refreshing. He sent me the finished front cover, which was beyond anything I had hoped for. Unfortunately, it was in color and I didn't realize copy machines don't reproduce color artwork well. I knew he had spent hours on the project and I hated to tell him it had to be in black and white. However when I did, Ricky simply said, "No problem. Just keep the one I sent for yourself and I'll do another."

I was amazed at Ricky's patience and his eagerness to help on the project. His artistic abilities astounded both Gary and me. He was twenty-three years old and had never had any art training, yet he could draw anything we asked. He had also written dozens of poems that were surprisingly good.

Ricky, Henry, Roberto, and Manuel all wrote articles. Jack Mazzan and Ricky sent me two poems each. Ricky not only redrew the front cover but designed one for the back as well.

Thomas Crump, one of the men from "The Hole" with whom I had been corresponding, sent me an incredible letter just before I received the articles and art from the others. I was so blessed by this letter that I wrote and asked Tom if I could have his permission to turn it into an article. I rewrote it, removing only the heading and personal references and sent it to Thomas for his approval.

In place of "Dear Jan and Gary" a bold banner read, "New Life!" and the article read:

> *I received a letter from a friend telling me how to ask Jesus into my heart. Now I'm a pretty tough guy and I have always felt that big men don't cry. Oh, I've expressed tears before, but to be crying on my knees and to have other people hear me is very unusual.*
>
> *I love Jesus and have asked Him to take me to heaven, maybe for the wrong reasons—I'm not sure. But as I read her letter and learned of her own heartaches, all in such a short period of time, I got cold all over and started to cry. I have for so many years been thinking of myself.*
>
> *I thought of her losing so many of her loved ones, yet she really cared about me. Really cared! I got down on my knees and asked Jesus to forgive me and take control of my life. I had run my life all these years and ruined it. God made me, and He knows what is best for me. I simply turned over control to Him.*
>
> *I couldn't hold back my tears. A guard came to my cell and asked me if I was all right. I told him the best yes I could at that moment, but he called the prison hospital and a guard and nurse came. They also asked me if I was all right. I was still crying and praying and I told them I was fine. The nurse asked if I wanted a sedative. I got up from my knees and walked to the door. I told her, "I don't need a sedative, I have Jesus! That's my sedative and my ticket to heaven!"*
>
> *All the guys were laughing at me, but she looked at me and said, "I'm sorry we bothered you, Tom." Never have I experienced anything like that in my life. I was never one who would take kindly to someone laughing at me, but that night I prayed for everyone here. They didn't make me mad. I honestly felt sorry for them.*

I can't explain everything I felt that night or what I am feeling now, but it's a feeling I wouldn't trade for anything in the world. Today the guys aren't laughing at me. At first they stared a little as I came out for my shower, and two guys asked me if I was all right. I told them Jesus made me feel just fine! They didn't want to hear that. I will pray for them.

I had a Friday I will never forget, and the people who really know me wouldn't believe it.

Thomas wrote back after he read the edited version and said, "I don't see anything wrong with that. Go ahead and print it if you want to. It's the truth!"

I didn't know how to type, and I didn't know the first thing about putting a newsletter together, but what I lacked in skill I made up for in determination. I sat down at the typewriter and laboriously pecked out the articles and poems with two fingers. My spelling was horrible, and I found myself looking up many words in the dictionary, which slowed the project down even more.

Finally, I had all the articles and poems ready for paste-up, but I needed artwork to dress them up a bit. I went to our local art store but they didn't have any Christian clip art, so I leafed through old church bulletins and cannibalized them. After each article was finished to my satisfaction, I checked on the price of paper, printing, and postage. I found to my dismay as I added up the figures that I was looking at a bill of $125. I knew there was no way we could afford it. The next day a friend of ours, Bud Wheeler, came to the store to take Gary to lunch. As he was waiting for Gary to finish with a customer, we chatted and I explained my dilemma to him. He said, "Jan, I have a friend who is in the printing business. Let me give him a call. I think he will sell you the paper at cost, and you can use my copy machine to make all the copies you want."

The paper cost me eight dollars. That night I went to Bud's office. Within hours the completed pages were stapled, and the newsletter was ready to mail.

The next day our friend Mitch Fox dropped off a roll of stamps. He said, "I know you're writing close to 150 letters a month. I thought you could use these. God provided Kitty and me with a little extra this month, and we wanted to share it with you." I used them to mail *The Rising Son*. God had our project figured out to the penny! After I mailed *The Rising Son* I had exactly eight dollars left in stamps—exactly what the paper had cost us.

In March, 1986, six days after we mailed *The Rising Son*, the mail started pouring in from inmates we had never met or written to. Almost everyone liked it. Several wrote and told me they wanted to write an article or poem for the next issue. I looked up and said, "What next issue, Lord?"

The owners of the Better Business Bureau, next door to our store, said, "We think what you are doing is great. We would like to provide the paper for the next issue, and you can use our copy machine." Again I lifted my eyes and repeated, "What next issue, Lord?"

As we prepared articles for volume 1, issue 2 of *The Rising Son*, we realized a full-fledged ministry was developing. We were no longer just two people writing a few letters of encouragement. I had promised the Lord I would walk through any door He opened. I knew He had turned a key, but I was afraid to step through the portal.

I held up my hand and said, "Walk with me, Father. I don't have the skills necessary to achieve what You are asking of me. Your Word tells me You delight in giving wisdom. I'll have the grit to climb the highest mountain for you Lord, if you'll supply the backpack."

After much soul searching and prayer we decided to name the ministry "Arms of Love," because that described what we do best. We reach out with arms of love and love everyone no one else wants to love.

Within a short time we discovered another local ministry had chosen the same name, so we joined forces. They handled outreach to convalescent centers and we led prison ministry. We discovered their convalescent ministry paralleled ours in one respect: old people are trapped in the prison of worn-out bodies and forgotten by family and friends.

The second issue of *The Rising Son* was full of surprises. It contained articles from six new authors on Nevada's death row and an article from a woman named Marie who was on death row in New Jersey. The editors of *The Dove Cage* who had helped advise us in putting together the first issue of *The Rising Son* ran a small ad in their magazine which read:

NEW DEATH ROW MAGAZINE!

Janalee and Gary Hoffman, along with the brothers on Nevada's row, have started a great new newsletter called The Rising Son. The first issue was truly inspirational. Write: The Rising Son, 1829 East Charleston, #100, Las Vegas, NV 89104.

Marie was the first person to respond to the ad. Along with a letter she enclosed a short article of encouragement for the men, which we printed in the second issue. Marie was the first woman we heard from on death row. Since then we have published articles written by four other death row females. Although we have received letters from most of the women who are condemned to die, only these five have submitted articles.

Each of the women that we have heard from is a professing Christian. The discovery that Jesus loves them and their accounts of holding Bible studies with each other are heart warming. It seems that the greatest punishment these women have received is not the sentence of death, but rather the separation from their children.

Had we known at the beginning *The Rising Son* would be more than a one-time effort and that women from death row would be writing for us, we undoubtedly would have chosen a different name for the newsletter. The men were deeply moved by Marie's article. Within a month our mailing list grew from thirty-eight to 152 subscribers. Marie was corresponding with people all over the country, in and out of prison. A good share of our new readers came through her. She sent them our name and address and told them about our newsletter. They would then write and ask us to place their names on our mailing list.

By the third issue our mailing list had grown to four hundred subscribers in thirty-eight prisons. Volume 1, issue 3 contained articles from death row inmates in New Jersey, Texas, South Dakota, Arkansas, Tennessee, and Louisiana, in addition to the eight articles submitted by those on Nevada's row. Our mailing list wasn't the only thing growing. So was the size of the newsletter!

We were again offered the use of a copy machine at no charge. But with the amount of paper we needed and the postage, we were looking at a bill of $150. Gary and I discussed it and decided to take a step in faith and do all the necessary functions to prepare it for printing. When God supplied our needs, it would be ready.

Business was slower than usual at the store so I was using the tops of the jewelry cases as tables to do the final paste-up for the newsletter. I had about five minutes of labor left on my project when Carrie and Dave Sumner stopped in to say hello. Carrie gave her heart to the Lord one week after Gary did. They were about our age and always had a quick smile and a kind word for everyone—the type of people we hoped to get to know better. Carrie sat down at the counter in front of me while

Dave and Gary visited on the couch. Carrie asked what I was doing. I carefully explained the ministry's attempt to bring the men on death row together as the Body of Christ through a newsletter they were authoring. I was the glue that put the pages together.

Carrie asked, "Now how does this work? Do you send this to them and they have it printed?" I said, "No Carrie, we've taken on the full responsibility of the project. They wouldn't have any way of printing it. It's all ready to print, and as soon as the Lord provides the funds we'll print and mail it." Carrie looked at me strangely and said, "Would you accept a little donation?" I was somewhat uncomfortable with that question. Always being a giver, I had difficulty being a receiver. But I smiled and said, "Sure, we'd really appreciate your help."

Carrie reached for her checkbook, placed it on her lap, and started to write. In my mind I figured she would write a check for five or ten dollars. I was rejoicing and sent up a silent prayer of thanks.

Carrie looked up with tears in her eyes and handed me a check for $150. She said, "The Lord told me to take care of it. Is this enough?"

After they left, Gary and I hugged each other. We were beginning to learn the power of faith. I realized that God waits patiently, asking only that we trust Him—even when we're not sure!

CHAPTER FIVE
Grace Blisters

"Commit your way to the Lord; trust in Him and He will do this: He will make your righteousness shine like the dawn, the justice of your cause like the noon day sun."

Psalms 37:5,6

What started as an attempt to bring the men on Nevada's death row together in the Body of Christ ultimately resulted in bringing the entire nation's death row population of Christians together. Gary and I felt overwhelmed by the number of letters we received each month. By the fourth issue our mailing list had grown to six hundred subscribers. We tried to answer most letters, but we couldn't possibly keep up with them all. On my knees I'd plead, "Lord, I can't take on one more pen pal."

Then I'd receive a letter from someone like Johnny in Texas. His next-door cell mate wrote and told me Johnny was lonely and he thought *The Rising Son* would be an encouragement to him. I sent Johnny a copy with a few words of encouragement. He wrote back and said, "My family lives within seventy-five miles of this prison. I have been on death row six years. In that time I have never had a visit, and your letter and newsletter are the first mail I've ever received!"

Gary and I did all the work ourselves on the newsletter. After the printing was completed, we collated, folded, stapled, and labeled the newsletters, and finally, licked stamps. All the addresses were typed on a sheet of paper, then cut apart and glued to each newsletter.

We couldn't keep borrowing copy machines from people. One Sunday morning I went to the altar during prayer time and said, "Father, we need a cheap copy machine—in fact, we need a free one."

Two day's later the death row inmates in San Quentin gave us a professional printing press! Bylle and Barbara Payton of Dove Flight Ministries wrote and said, "The Lord provided this press for us to use in printing *The Dove Cage*. We have never used it because it requires a professional printer to run it. After we got it, a printing company offered to print *The Dove Cage* free of charge, including the paper. The owner is a Christian, and he discovered it ministered to his employees. The Lord provided it to us for prison ministry. We can't give it to you, but it is yours to use for as long as you print *The Rising Son*."

"Lord," I said with a look of suspicion on my face, "I distinctly remember asking you for a cheap little copy machine. Excuse me for saying so, but giving us a professional printing press tends to make me a little nervous of Your intentions!"

Within two years our mailing list swelled to over two thousand subscribers. By the end of the third year we had more than four thousand and reached 152 prisons in the U.S.A. and prisons in twenty-seven foreign countries. Inmates were requesting copies for family and friends. Ministers were requesting it to use in their jail and prison ministries. Our first requests from foreign countries came from Mexico, Canada, England, and Brazil. Gary's editorials are always fun and lighthearted. In one of them he wrote:

> *It's not enough that I now have friends called Ewok, Singing Dave, KiKi, Castro, Killer, Sonshine, Super Glue, and Anonymous. It's not enough that we have eight kids of our own. But now my wife has adopted two*

thousand more on the row all over the United States and four foreign countries. We just received a letter from Brazil. I'll tell you right now, if I get one collect call from Rio de Janeiro, I'm going to rip out all the phones!

Because the ministry was growing at such a tremendous rate, Gary and I knew we would need a board of directors to help us make decisions, so we formed a corporation. With much regret we separated from Arms of Love Ministry and incorporated under the name Rising Son Ministry because it was already a known entity.

Our home church played an immense roll in our growth. As we printed our sixth issue the church family rallied around us and helped us with collating, folding, stapling, and preparing *The Rising Son* for mailing. Together we learned a lot about grace blisters and holy sweat! Many members helped with donations for postage and other necessities. It takes nearly five hundred man hours to put each issue together. Without our church family we couldn't have continued.

Lay people from around the country wanted to help. Our greatest need was for Christians to become pen pals. We helped over 250 people start pen-friend ministries. I sent one couple the birth dates of people on death row, and they sent them each a birthday card. For many on the row it was the only mail they had ever received. By continuing to send birthday cards, Connie and her family show the men that someone cares, and that Jesus cares.

As our circulation grew, we began to receive mail from others who were ministering to prisoners on death row. We discovered Bill Wall of Hattiesburg, Mississippi, has a fantastic correspondence ministry to dozens of men on death rows all over the country. It was wonderful to know someone else was experiencing our same joys and frustrations in this difficult ministry. Bill is a tremendous source of advice and encouragement.

He introduced us to George and Ann Gaines who have written hundreds of letters to prisoners on death row, sharing Christ's love. Whereas I write most of the letters in our ministry, George is the main correspondent in theirs, and he does it all from a wheelchair. He was sixty-nine years old when they began their "Life Row Ministries."

Because of the deterioration of George's health, their daughter has taken over most of the correspondence, but George continues to participate as much as he is able. Over the years, they have sent hundreds of cassette tape players along with Gospel teaching tapes to prisoners on the row. These prisoners are not allowed to go to the chapel, so Life Row Ministries delivers the chapel to them.

Another death row ministry in Oklahoma publishes a monthly newsletter and corresponds with many inmates. One day the director sent me a letter he had received, saying, "I thought this might be a blessing to you." The letter read:

Dear friends,

You asked me how I got saved. Well, I was sitting here one night listening to some of the guys talk and someone slid a copy of The Rising Son down the runway between our cells and I reached out and grabbed it. I read every word. I enjoyed it. Some of the stories really got to me, and I realized I was living the wrong lifestyle. I got down on my knees and prayed very hard for God to forgive me for all of my sins and to come into my life. I asked Him to show me how to live my life for Him and to serve Him. I prayed He would change my life and make me a better man.

Robert

Through the message of salvation, our ministries are working in harmony with each other, turning death row into life row! This has shown Gary and I the importance of the Body of Christ working together for God's glory.

God astounds me at times in the unique way He answers prayer. One morning as I drove to work, after being up for several nights until 3:00 A.M. to get *The Rising Son* ready for print, I said, "Lord, I'm weary! I know you don't mean this ministry to drain me. I need help, Father, I can't go on pushing myself like this. Could you find someone to help carry the load?"

As I unlocked the doors of the store the phone rang. A lady from church named LaWanda White said, "Jan, I know you don't know me well, but I want to donate some time to serving God, and I wondered if you could use some help? Perhaps I could answer some letters. Could I be of help to you?"

"Oh, thank you, Jesus!" I whispered as I looked up and winked. LaWanda became one of my dearest friends and one of my greatest answers to prayer. She not only answered hundreds of letters, she also typed a good share of the articles for *The Rising Son*. Her tender and compassionate heart offered insights and encouragement I desperately needed.

One day I complained because I had received some harsh letters. My feelings were bruised. LaWanda said, "Jan, when everyone is happy with a person in ministry, it is because that person is compromising the Word of God. Rejoice when you have a few that are snapping at your heels."

After a year LaWanda and her husband Buryl moved to California to be close to their son. I knew of the planned move for months. Yet when the day came for good-byes, my heart was heavy. Her motherly wisdom and insights will never be forgotten.

Although she lives hundreds of miles away, LaWanda still remains a vital part of this ministry. She continues to counsel and encourage me through her letters and phone calls. In her most recent letter she wrote:

> *I still believe prison ministries are "last days" ministries, and I also remember that in the last days the "very elect" will be deceived if possible. Take courage my dear one. Stand firm. I have a feeling you are a plum Satan would just love to have on his thumb and say, "What a good boy am I."*
>
> *I pray a hedge of protection around you, and you dare not lay down the shield of faith for a second. Satan would delight in discouraging you, but remember what God said to Joshua: "Have I not commanded you? Be strong and courageous. Do not be terrified; do not be discouraged, for the Lord your God will be with you wherever you go" (Joshua 1:9).*
>
> *Go with God my dear, dear friend. I love and miss you so much.*
>
> *LaWanda*

I've found the Lord never takes something from us without replacing it. He sent Dandy Hughes to stand in the gap. She is a tenacious Christian who delights in taking on the difficult inmates who write to us. I delight in placing them in her capable hands. Although blessed with the gift of mercy, she handles adversity well.

Some prisoners provided a tremendous source of help and encouragement to us. Henry hounded the men to get their articles in on time, and Ricky had a wealth of ideas for the cover art. With each issue his art work improved. My favorite among Ricky's covers is the one of Jesus standing behind a set of bars with half His face showing, and His hand crushing the metal bars He holds. In the pupil of His eye is the reflection of the cross. Another favorite is a drawing of a prison yard, surrounded by fence and razor wire. Beyond the fence is a mountain dotted with homes. Over the mountain is a glorious sunrise. What made the drawing most spectacular was the melting bars on the window of the cell, that can be seen as one looks out the cell window from within.

As we got to know Ricky better, we learned his mother had thrown him out of the house when he was only twelve years old while divorcing her second husband. She had remarried and her new husband had no use for him. Ricky's father had also remarried. His new wife had children of her own and didn't want responsibility for Ricky either. Ricky ended up living with his grandmother because she was the only one who cared enough to take him in.

Ricky became a little wayfaring stranger, wandering the country. My heart ached for this lost boy. He was one of our nation's thrown away children. Ricky was desperately lonely, and more than anything wanted a mother's approval, but he knew that approval would never come. She wrote him off and never contacted him after his arrest—not even when she knew he was condemned to die. Ricky became our new son. If she didn't want him, we knew someone who did—us!

In August, 1986 we received a letter postmarked Nashville, Tennessee, from a man named Gerald Laney. Gerald couldn't read or write, but a cell mate named Kenny, wrote for him. Gerald shared a powerful testimony that astounded Gary and me:

> *When I was a child the teachers made fun of me because I couldn't read or write. As hard as I tried I couldn't make sense of those words or numbers. (I had dyslexia but no one recognized it at the time.)*

The teacher thought I wasn't making an effort so to punish me she would draw a circle on the blackboard and make me stand with my nose in the middle of it. When I went out to play with the other kids at recess time, the teacher put signs on my back. The other kids would either shun me or make fun of me.

I started cutting school and hanging out with older guys at the pool hall. The pool hall served as a social hall for the area bikers. I would sweep up to make a little spending money. I learned those guys were somebody, because they were bad. No one messed with them. No one ridiculed or made fun of them. I didn't fit in at school, but I was accepted here as one of them.

As time went on and I grew, I was accepted into a motorcycle gang called the "Ghost Riders." I worked my way up to the rank of enforcer and after several years I became the national enforcer for seven chapters of the Ghost Riders. Once, I burned down a Hell's Angels clubhouse once because they owed us some money for drugs.

A businessman from our community was in debt to our club for some pot he had purchased. He paid one thousand dollars and he owed the same amount. He said he wasn't going to pay, so they sent me to either collect or scare the guy.

I waited in his driveway until he drove up. He stepped from his car and I screamed, "Hey, you owe us some money, I'm here to collect."

What I didn't know was the Ghost Riders had been threatening him. He was expecting someone to show up. He turned, and I saw a flash of his gun as he aimed and fired. He shot me four times before I got off a single shot. I was hit in the side, the leg, and directly on my ear. He lay dead in the driveway. An ambulance was called and I was rushed to the nearest medical center.

As my father and mother entered the hospital the doctor told them there was a good chance I wouldn't live and, even if I did, I would in all probability be a vegetable for the rest of my life. The police who waited outside the door informed them if I recovered I would be charged with murder.

As they approached the emergency room table where I lay, my mother touched my legs—they were ice cold. As this happened, I was drifting out of my body. I could see the tubes sticking into my body and the doctors and nurses working over me. I drifted above the hospital and over the parking lot. I could see the water tower that loomed over the city growing smaller. I started shooting past the stars at an astronomical speed. I entered through what appeared to be a black cloud and felt myself falling. I saw what I thought was the sun. It was about the size of a quarter. I could hear people screaming and I smelled a horrible putrid smell. As I got closer to the sun, I realized it was a pit of fire and the smell was of burning flesh. I recalled my father and grandmother telling me if I didn't get my heart right with God I would die and go to hell. Was I going to hell?

My father, who is a minister, cradled my head in his hands and started to pray as my mother touched my cold legs. "Lord, You've let us have him this long, please don't take him yet," he prayed. They both knew they were losing me. He said my head vibrated in his hands. As they prayed over me I started moving away from that burning pit at the same speed that took me there. I was moving so fast as I passed through the ceiling of the emergency room that I thought I would splat all over the table, but instead I just drifted into my body. I opened my eyes and said, "Oh Dad, please don't let me go back to sleep!" I was afraid I would go back to hell.

I was tried, convicted, and sentenced to death. I was placed on Tennessee's death row. My health began to slowly deteriorate because of poor medical attention. I could do little more than drag my leg behind me, and I had lost a considerable amount of weight.

Because of the wound in my thigh, my circulation was bad and the prison doctor told me I could lose my leg. He made a brace for my leg, but I refused to use it. To me that was like admitting defeat!

One Sunday morning I awoke early and started flipping the TV channels, looking for something other than preachers preaching. Finally I gave up and decided to watch one of them until something of interest came on. The preacher said, "If you want a spiritual or a physical healing, as a sign of faith, place your hand on the TV."

I was afraid to walk to the television set. What if one of the men walked by and saw me? I hated to be ridiculed, but finally I lay my hand on that set. It was like a shot of electricity going through my body. I knew I was healed!

One day a chaplain came up to my cell. I had talked to him several times, and I knew from the other men he could be trusted. Some ministers were nothing more than another badge, but Frank really cared. I said, "Frank, something happened to me that I have never shared with anyone before for fear they would think I was making it up or they would laugh at me. I need to tell someone— can I trust you not to laugh?" Frank assured me he wouldn't. I told him of my brush with hell and the healing that took place when I trusted God enough to lay my hand on the TV, to show my faith.

Frank told me, "Gerald, there is a name for what happened to you when you felt yourself going to hell. You had what is called a near death experience. You aren't the only person to claim this has happened, but you are the only one I know of who was headed for hell. Most claim to see a beautiful white light they describe as love. You need to share this story with others. It is a special *testimony that God allowed you to have. He wants you to use it to bring others to salvation."*

Gerald became a regular contributor to *The Rising Son*, with Kenny as his scribe, until the two of them were separated. Kenny got sick and was taken to the prison's infirmary.

One day I received a letter from another man in Tennessee named Steve West. Enclosed with the letter was an article entitled, "How I Met the Enforcer!"

Steve told of being in the maximum security area of death row where new inmates were placed and where troublemakers were housed. Because of the lack of privileges, all the men on the tier had rebelled against the guards. They threw food trays at them and kept their cells filthy. Steve went along with the system and didn't make waves. Because he didn't cooperate with the inmates, they made threats on his life. Steve was moved to the prison hospital for safe keeping until there was an opening in a safer unit.

The men in Unit 1 circulated a rumor that Steve was a snitch. He was told the biggest inmate in Unit 6 would kill him. This adversary was a friend of the men Steve had just left. Steve was scared for a good reason. Being labeled a snitch, whether true or false, is one of the greatest reasons people are killed in prison.

The day Steve was moved to Unit 6 all the others were out in the yard. He discovered the man called "The Enforcer" not only lived in that unit, but he was the "Rock Man." The Rock Man is in charge of cleanup for the unit he lives in. That meant he would be out on the walk that passed each cell door.

One by one the men were brought in from the yard, allowed to shower, and placed back in their cells—with the exception of The Enforcer who was left on the walk. Steve said a silent prayer for it was no exaggeration that he was the biggest man there. Steve said, "Lord, You allowed me to be placed here, and I trust that You are in control of this situation as I meet my adversary."

As the giant man walked up to his cell Steve said, "Look, if we are going to have trouble let's get it over with right now." The Enforcer looked at Steve and said, "What makes you think we have a problem?" With a glint in his eyes he sized up Steve's thin frame and walked away.

Steve scanned his empty cell in search of something he could use as a weapon to defend himself. He knew The Enforcer would return. Sure enough, moments later the massive hulk of a man stepped up to his cell and reached through the bars. He handed Steve some copies of *The Rising Son* and other Christian literature. He asked, "How's your relationship with Christ?" In his astonishment Steve replied, "Well I have a personal relationship with Christ if that is what you are asking, but it's difficult to be a Christian in prison." Steve discovered Gerald Laney was still The Enforcer, but now he was the enforcer for Jesus Christ!

Steve has a brilliant mind and is a gifted writer. In addition to helping Gerald answer his mail and write articles for *The Rising Son*, Steve is helping Gerald write an autobiography.

Steve himself became a regular writer for *The Rising Son*. As we corresponded over the months he told me he was an illegitimate child. His mother married while he was young, and while seperated from her husband, became pregnant with Steve. He was a constant reminder to his stepfather of his mother's infidelity. He was the outlet for his stepfather's wrath and was subjected to almost daily beatings. The battered child could possibly have endured the abusive treatment had his mother offered her love and comfort, but she treated him with the same contempt.

In February, 1987 I was scheduled for meetings in Mississippi and Georgia. I made a side trip to the prison in Nashville to visit Steve, Gerald, and four other inmates. Gerald was indeed the giant Steve had described, but Steve was also a giant—the kind that looms taller inside than a small frame can contain.

Upon returning home from this memorable visit, we received an article from Steve for *The Rising Son*.

How many times have you heard prison called "Satan's Playground"? Without a doubt that is true. Even less of a doubt is death row containing enough evil to make the devil smile.

Most of the time this evil isn't combatted; it's nurtured to a frenzied extent: old Satan must be proud. But on occasion, things do transpire which must make him shriek in terror. One of these occasions is what I wish to share with you.

It was a day much like all days on the row: yard time, showers, chow, etc., but behind the scenes, six of the inmates were preparing for something beyond what even they could comprehend.

For days, hostility had run rampant over the row. Rumors and words had caused hatred to boil. What is more, these six men all knew of the surmounting problems. Satan was having his way with these—society's bad men. Only God knew how it would come out.

In the evening, each man was taken out of his cell and placed in the visiting room. Crowded together was at least eight death penalties and who knows how many years. A room where even the toughest of guards would fear walking.

But there was an angel present. Little Jan Hoffman had come to see these men. An angel in a room full of bad men whom Satan was toying with, yet no anxiety, hostility, or resentment dared rear its head. Jan brought with her the peace and love of God that spread over each man as he entered. Her eyes told us she loved us and her words told us that God did too.

We shared a few hours together, talking of God and His word. At the end, a joint prayer was said by everyone.

Frank, the prison's minister who had accompanied and escorted her put in his share of love, but mostly sat back and watched the love flow out of Jan into each of us.

That night, after lock down, the walk was brisk with conversation. The love that Jan brought to us spread throughout the row. You could feel the difference and know that the Holy Spirit was moving. The anger present before her visit had now left. No harsh words were spoken. Instead, the love and word of God now came into focus, causing each of the six to praise God.

Though this doesn't sound like much of a story, still there's a lesson to be learned. We're told in the Bible, to use Christ as our example in living a righteous Christian life. For many of us this is difficult, but with Jan entering Tennessee's death row and sharing her life of Christ with us, men were humbled, were called to repentance, and learned a deeper, more beautiful love of God.

Jan, each of us thanks you beyond words for what you gave us that day. You came to us as people, not inmates, and you let us know that we really are important because God loves us. Because of you, Satan lost a battle that he had been working on for quite some time.

So you see, brothers and sisters, everything you do and everything you say, do and say that which keeps our Father foremost. You'll never know when you're carrying a message as Jan was.

In no uncertain terms, an angel came to Tennessee's death row and released the bad men from the hands of Satan. We love you Jan. God bless you.

I was hesitant to use this article in *The Rising Son*, because Gary and I usually omit anything in submitted articles referring to us personally. The object of the newsletter is to bring glory to God—not us. However, after much prayer and discussion, Gary felt that there was a strong enough message in Steve's article and that over all, it did direct the glory to God, so we decided to print it.

On the back page of *The Rising Son* we have a mailing coupon for updating addresses or ordering our newsletter. On the bottom is a place for comments. Each day we receive several of them. Some of the more common comments are:

We have a jail ministry and The Rising Son is a wonderful witnessing tool. Keep up the good work.

I just read The Rising Son for the first time and I can see I'm not living my life right. I just want you to know I've dedicated my heart to the Lord!

I would like to have a Christian friend to write to. It's lonely here without someone to care about me.

I'd like to learn more about the Lord. Can you help?

I've been a Christian for six years and one month. It just gets better every day!

I am a twenty-one-year old man who has just begun his walk with Christ. I need a real friend to help guide me in the right direction!

One day we received a coupon from a man named Gary Davis that said, "Do you think God wants me?" Those six little words inspired a six-page letter from me:

Dear Gary,

> *There is nothing we can do that is so horrible that God will cast us into hell. There is nothing we can do that is so good that we can climb our way to heaven. Crawl up on God's lap and say, "I made it!" It is only by accepting or rejecting what Jesus did for us on the cross that will determine whether we go to heaven or hell.*
>
> *Let me ask you a question. "If you saw a brand new baby lying on the ground, filthy, cold, scraped, scratched, bruised, and hungry, would you make someone give that baby a bath before you picked it up? You wouldn't care about that dirt, would you? You'd just pick that dirty little baby up.*
>
> *Well Gary, that is the only way we can go to God—like dirty babies. If we will raise our hands to Him and call out, He will pick us up, warm us, feed us, fix all the places where we are scratched and bruised, and only then will He start to worry about the dirt. I think He would probably clean our faces first, so He could see the beauty He created. God will take that dirt (sin) off, one layer at a time. The same way it went on. Gary, just reach up to Him and call out His name. He loves you and He is waiting for you.*

Gary not only gave his heart to Christ, but he started ministering to a next-door neighbor through a quarter-size hole in between their cells. Each day they would hold Bible studies together and spend time in prayer.

One day Gary Davis wrote to me and said, "Sis, Frank Rodriguez lives next door to me. He is so lonely. No one ever writes to him. I know you are busy, but do you think you could drop him a few lines? I love him like a brother, and I know a letter would make him happy."

I began writing to Frank, and I sensed his deep loneliness. He was open and his sweet spirit was almost childlike. Frank shared many things that came straight from his heart—things he had never been able to share before. No one else had cared enough to listen. He wrote:

> *At the time I went to trial, my attorney went to visit my parents to ask them if they would go to court with me. My attorney suggested they might help prevent me from getting the death penalty. They told my attorney they never wanted to see me or talk to me again. I tried writing but they sent my letters back. I tried calling and they changed their phone number.*
>
> *I have a little brother who is also in this prison but not on the row. Every Saturday a guard comes to my cell door and says, "Hey Frank, I see your little brother got a visit today. Did your mom and dad come see you?" I never say anything. I just lay down on my bunk and feel bad. I haven't heard from one member of my family in two years.*

I wrote back and said, "Frank, I don't even know how old you are, but if your family doesn't want you, I know one that does. I'd be proud to be your mother or your sister. I'll let you choose what part of our family you'd like to be."

Frank wrote back, "Oh, my dearest Mother!"

Every Saturday the guard came to Frank's cell door and taunted him. Frank, being a new Christian, was eager to serve Christ and decided this guard would be his mission field. One Saturday the guard came to his door and said, "Ya, Frank, we have to do a shakedown on your cell. Step on out." A shakedown, Frank explained, is a time when the guards go into your cell and go through everything you own looking for contraband. When they leave you are stuck with cleaning up the mess. Some inmates call it "tossing a cell" because they toss the convict's belongings everywhere. They even read the personal letters they have saved and then throw them on the floor and walk on them.

This day they didn't chain Frank to the outside of his bars as they usually did. Instead two guards escorted Frank to a holding cell that looked over the visiting room. Frank wrote to me, "Mother, I hurt until I couldn't hurt anymore. I sat there watching my family visiting my brother. They were hugging, laughing, and having a grand time with each other. Finally they took me back to my cell. Gary and I crouched near to the hole between our cells and he got me calmed down. I know that guard did that on purpose!"

I wrote back and said, "Son, there is a story in the Bible about Lazarus and a rich man (Luke 16:19-25). Lazarus was a poor beggar who laid at the rich man's gate longing to eat what fell from the rich man's table. Even the dogs came and licked his sores. The time came when the angels carried him to Abraham's side. The rich man also died and was buried. In hell where he was in torment he looked up and saw Abraham far away with Lazarus at his side. So he called to him, 'Father Abraham, have pity on me and send Lazarus to dip the tip of his finger in water and cool my tongue because I'm in agony in this fire.' But Abraham replied, 'Son, remember that in your lifetime you received your good things, while Lazarus received bad things, but now he is comforted and you are in agony.'

Son, every time this guard comes to your cell, why don't you offer him a cup of water? He'll probably turn it down each time, but maybe some day he will ask you why you are offering it to him. That will give you an opportunity to share this story. You can also tell him about the "living water" that Jesus offers. If he turns down

Christ's living water, there may come a day when he calls out, 'Father Abraham, send Frank to dip his finger in water to cool my tongue.' When Abraham tells him he already had the good things in life, perhaps he will remember all the cups of water you offered that he turned down."

Gary and I sent Frank a Bible. His name was printed in gold, and we wrote an inscription inside the first page. We signed it, "With our love, Mom and Dad."

God surely has a sense of humor because it was Frank's tormentor who delivered it to him. As the guard was inspecting it at Frank's door, looking for saw blades or drugs, he read the inscription and asked Frank who sent him the Bible. Frank went and got a picture we had sent him and said, "My Mom and Dad sent it!" Frank wrote, "Mother, that guard just looked at me funny, shook his head and walked away."

Just recently as this guard was walking by his cell he said in passing, "Oh, by the way Frank, your mother is in a coma and they don't expect her to live!" With that comment he went on his way.

Frank asked to see Chaplain Ben, a dear godly Christian chaplain at the prison. After checking, he told Frank his mother had died.

Just like clockwork the guard was back at Frank's cell door the following Saturday. "Frank, did you hear the good news? Your old man hired guards for your brother so he could go to your mother's funeral!"

On my last birthday I received a check in the amount of $100. I thought I might buy a new dress for a chaplains' conference I was invited to attend with the unexpected windfall, but I knew I should give it to Gary to help with some bills that needed to be paid.

I just couldn't bring myself to cash that check. I should have given it to Gary, but I didn't want to do that. I knew as the days passed I didn't want the dress either. My quandary was not knowing how to tell Gary what I really wanted to do with that $100. As we drove to Gary's mother's house for Sunday night dinner I said, "Gary, can I do anything I want with my birthday money?"

He took his eyes off the road, glanced at me and said, "Sure, it's yours. Do what ever will make you happy, Jan."

In a timid voice I asked, "Can I give it away?" Without hesitation he said, "If that's what you want—do it!"

Feeling I needed to explain, I said, "You know Frank is locked down twenty-three hours a day with nothing to help him pass the time. He has no TV or radio and he has no money. He can't even buy a stick of deodorant or a bottle of shampoo. If he wants to shampoo his hair he either has to use a bar of soap or borrow from Gary Davis. Gary shares all his toiletries freely with him and never complains, but Frank hates to ask when he knows Gary has so little. It would give me so much pleasure to send the money to Frank and let him buy himself some items he needs."

Gary grinned and said, "Then send it!"

Gary and I try to help with a real need when we are able, but we never provide luxuries such as a TV. With the vast number of inmates we write to, we've learned if you buy something for one, you'd better be prepared to buy for everyone, especially when they live in the same prison. Like children, they feel hurt or slighted. This situation was different. Frank had never known Christian love and we wanted to make up for the tyrannical behavior of the guard. We wanted to show him Christ's love in action.

As luck—or God's timing—would have it, that TV was delivered on a Saturday afternoon. The only day Frank's tormentor worked on that unit. As he walked up to Frank's door he snarled, "Where did you get the money for a TV?" Frank grinned and said, "From my Mom and Dad!"

Gary and I received a long distance phone call from the director of chaplaincy ministries for our church. He invited us to be chaplains on his volunteer staff. I said, "Chaplain Bowers, neither Gary nor I is an ordained minister. We have a local minister's license, but that is all."

Chaplain Bowers said, "You may not have a sheepskin hanging on your wall, but you are ministers. You have been anointed by the finger of God as He wrote on the walls of your hearts!"

I'm not very comfortable using the title chaplain, but it has opened the doors for us to visit in several death rows around the country. Although we seldom use the title, the bonus to being on Chaplain Bowers's staff is the advice and encouragement we receive, and especially the opportunity to give accountability, which we believe is important for anyone in ministry.

There will be more reflection of Christ in our lives if there is more reflection on Him! God doesn't care about our abilities or our circumstances in life. He wants us to bloom where we are planted. He wants to use each of us.

Molly thought God could never use her, and yet, she has added a new ingredient to her cookie dough, love! Carolyn Clark, a member of my church, is a hairdresser. She goes to a nursing home or the hospital one day a week. She washes, cuts, and sets the patients' hair. She not only beautifies the patients' outward appearance, but she shows them with her love they also have souls that are crying for a beauty make-over.

We have seen death row inmates who are chained, contained, and locked away from all of society laboring for Christ. Numerous men on death row have a ministry to young people. They write dozens of letters each month from their prison cells to troubled youth who are headed down the wrong road. They are teaching them the dangers of drugs, alcohol, wrong choices, and wrong friends.

Gary Davis has a ministry writing to alcoholics. Frank Rodriguez has a ministry to a guard who torments him. To me that is a supreme act of love for Christ.

One day an inmate offered Frank a joint of grass as an officer's back was turned. Frank, who had been a drug addict, could have smoked it or sold it for necessities he desperately needed. Instead he said, "No thanks, I get high on Jesus now! That's a high I never have to come down from! You should try it some time."

Cary Williams and Henry Dawson start each day in prayer, "Father, how do you want to use me today? Show me!" That's a prayer request God will never deny. Ricky Sechrest and Jeff Farmer use their talents as artists to bring glory to God. Bill Wall has helped Gerald Laney produce a tract which has been sent all over the U.S.A. and is now sent to foreign countries.

Because death row prisoners are willing to take a public stand for Christ in *The Rising Son*, their testimonies have led hundreds of lost souls home. They are locked in, but the love of God cannot be locked out.

A young prisoner in our jail who was facing the death penalty read a copy of *The Rising Son* that he found in the day room. He wrote:

> *I am in jail with a good possibility of going to "life row." The brothers and sisters on life row have comforted me with their poems and testimonies. God's Word is the best medicine money "can't" buy. I love the Lord and have come to find out He is like a garbage recycler. The trash man, (Satan), dumps all the garbage at the dump, but before he can plow it into the ground, the Recycler, (Jesus Christ), searches vigorously to find all that has value or worth. What man thought wasn't salvageable, He found to be hidden treasure. He sends it through a fire to make it new and to purify it.*

1 praise God for making me new and filling me with love and joy.

My brothers and sisters on death row, my heart is with you and 1 want you to know you've inspired me to keep on going. You've shown me a whole new way to serve Christ. 2 Corinthians 6:4-5 tells us no matter where we are or what we are doing, we are to be ministers of God through Jesus Christ.

CHAPTER SIX
Where Angels Shout!

*"My sheep hear my voice, and I know them, and they follow me:
And I give unto them eternal life; and they shall never perish,
neither shall any man pluck them out of my hand."*

John 10:27,28, KJV

Looking out the third story window of the hotel, Gary
and I could see the state capitol building. It was April,
1987. Huge trees adorned the grounds with grace and
beauty. Snow still blanketed their otherwise bare limbs.
Large stately homes dotted the city like guardians, with
lights twinkling in the windows to cheer the night. Carson
City is a quaint hamlet nestled in the foothills of the Sierra
Nevada mountains in the northwest corner of Nevada.
The majestic mountains loomed like giants in the
background.

Yet, directly in front of us, we could see the glaring
floodlights that surround the century-old prison. The
presence of the prison belied the sleepy hollow effect of
the city because it housed over five hundred of the state's
most dangerous convicts. Because of excitement over our
next day's visit to the prison, I knew it would be a long
night without much sleep. I recalled the series of events
that culminated to this day.

After our second mailing of *The Rising Son*, we received
a letter from the warden at Nevada State Prison. It said:

June 13, 1986

Dear Mr. & Mrs. Hoffman,

    This letter is in regards to your publication, The Rising Son, a Christ-centered publication by death row inmates. We feel this publication is inappropriate. We would request from your organization that you cease publishing material from our inmates at the Nevada State Prison. We would greatly appreciate your assistance and cooperation regarding this matter.

This letter was signed by the warden. Gary and I were stunned! What could possibly be more appropriate than sharing Christ with people who were about to meet Him? They could have all the girlie magazines they wanted but not this Christian newsletter?

Gary and I weren't sure what the men's constitutional rights were with regard to the publication, but we knew our First Amendment rights were being violated.

We talked to the volunteer chaplain who we were serving with at the Jean facility to see if she was familiar with the legalities concerning inmates writing for *The Rising Son.* She called Nevada's attorney general to find out. He said, "The state's prison director and the warden called a meeting in my office to see what the warden could do about squashing this publication. I told them to do nothing until they heard from me. I wanted to read this "Rambo" material for myself before I made a decision on the matter. I have just read both issues of *The Rising Son,* and they are sensitive and well-done. Tell those people from Arms of Love Ministry to keep printing. They won't have any problems from the prison. Oh, and by the way, would you ask them to put me on the mailing list?"

Eight men expressed their desire to be baptized, but because there was no chaplain in their prison, they were concerned that it would never be a reality. We made an appointment to see the state's governor to find out if there was some way for them to be baptized. When we confronted him with our dilemma he said, "Why don't you go baptize them yourselves?"

We explained the letter we had received from the warden with regard to *The Rising Son*, and the reply we received from the attorney general. We told him we didn't think the warden would welcome us with open arms.

The governor said, "Well, I appoint the jobs of warden and prison director, so I carry a little clout with them. I'll set up an appointment for you to visit the state prison director and I'll send my personal aide with you to take notes and report back to me."

I opened our jewelry store while Gary kept the appointment with the director. When he came back he was beaming. He said we would be allowed to go into the prison and see anyone on the row we wanted. The first trip would be an introductory visit. We would be allowed to do the baptisms on the second visit if all went well with the first. What started out as an attack by Satan to exterminate *The Rising Son* and keep it out of the prison became an open door to ministry.

The next day I felt refreshed. This was the Lord's special day. Though I've never been a breakfast person, Gary encouraged me to eat a good morning meal. "It's going to be a long day, Jan, and you'll need something nourishing to sustain you." I made an effort to eat, but in reality I only pushed the food around on my plate. I discovered if you push your food to the outer rim of the plate and leave a big empty gap in the middle, it looks as though you've at least eaten something. Although I didn't eat much, I made up for it with the coffee I drank trying to wake up. No matter how many times I looked at my watch, it didn't seem to move on this Good Friday morning. Finally Gary said, "Okay, lets go!"

Inside the prison guard station, a woman was already waiting for a visit with her husband Tom. She inquired politely, "Are you Jan and Gary Hoffman?" We smiled and nodded. She introduced herself as Vicki and said, "The guys on the row asked me to deliver a little gift to you from them." From behind her back she pulled out a beautiful orchid corsage. She hugged me and said, "Happy Easter to you from them."

We waited our turn to pass through the metal detector. Once on the other side, the guard carefully inspected the Bible I had carried in. The warden had okayed the Bible, a silver dish, and a small silver pouring pitcher.

As I once again stepped into the small closet-size room for the pat search, even the corsage was inspected. Janet winked at me and said, "It's beautiful, you must be proud."

The guards on the "goon squad" escorted the men from CMU to the visiting room. The goon squad, as the men call them, are comparable to what we would call a "swat team" on the streets. When there is a major shakedown of the prisoner's cells, they are in charge. At the slightest sign of trouble inside the prison walls the goon squad is rushed to that area of dissension wearing full riot gear.

These transporting guards grumbled to the visiting room officers the whole time they were escorting the men, "There's sure to be a hostage situation here. Someone is going to get hurt. You just mark my words!" Janet and Mike, the guards in charge of the visiting room, shooed them out the door saying, "Let us worry about the hostages," nodding at Gary and me.

"We have less problems with the men from the condemned unit than any other part of the prison," Janet said. "Don't let his bad temper spoil your day."

The prisoners who had requested a visit with us were all brought in at one time. We were to have them all for the whole day! We had thought we would have three or four men at a time for two hours; that was the way the warden had arranged the visit.

Gary and I wondered if the goon squad had deliberately tried to set up a crisis situation. We knew we weren't in any danger, but they were convinced we were gullible fools.

Eight men in the group had submitted "kites" to the warden, requesting Gary and I baptize them. We were placed in a room beside the regular visiting area. There were sixteen of us, as the non-Christian men who requested a visit joined us.

We could be seen through a big glass window the whole time by Janet, but there were no overhead cameras, and none of the guards came into the room the whole six hours. Ricky Sechrest's friend, Charlie Wessels, had come to visit him and Janet allowed Charlie to join us.

Everyone was so excited at the unexpected turn of events that we all talked at one time. We loved them, and we had no doubt we were loved. It was an irony. Here we were in a room filled with people considered so dangerous that they were locked away from other murderers. It felt like a family reunion rather than a visit with the condemned. Not once did we entertain the idea of being in danger. The truth is, no one would have dared hurt either of us.

After a few hours of visiting, we shared the story of John the Baptist baptizing Jesus, and we talked about the importance of baptism. We asked the men who wished to be baptized if they would come forward.

My husband Gary stepped up first and said, "I am a Jew by birth. I became a Christian two years ago on Easter Sunday. I have never been baptized. We recently had a baptismal service at our church, but I decided to wait because I wanted to be baptized with you men. I can't think of anything that would be more meaningful for me."

With that Gary handed me the silver pitcher the guard had filled with water, and the long-denied baptisms began.

I stuck my head out the door and asked Janet if the inmate who took the photographs could join us. With a smile Janet said, "No problem, I'll send him right in."

Don was the first to step forward. We had requested to see him alone as we had on the first visit. The guards were to return him to his cell before the other men were transported, but they left Don behind. He had made a lot of enemies with his bullying tactics. Some of the men were uncomfortable with his presence in the room. Gary and I could feel their uneasiness. They were afraid Don would "go off" and they were watching guardedly, as much to protect us as each other.

Gary had spent a considerable amount of time talking to Don before the others arrived. "Don," Gary said, "you have to walk that walk if you are going to talk that talk. It costs nothing to become a Christian, but it costs everything to live the Christian life. Jesus said we are to count the cost if we are going to be His followers. You had better get your calculator out."

Don cleared his throat nervously as his eyes scanned each face, "I have hurt a lot of you with my past actions and attitudes. I'm sorry for all I've done, and I ask your forgiveness. I promise I will try to do better in the future. I don't know if I'll be successful, but I promise I'll try my best with Jesus' help. I know if I claim to be a Christian, I must live like one, and I haven't done a very good job of it. I would like to be baptized with you today."

Gary held the silver dish to catch the water as I poured. "I baptize you Don, in the name of the Father, and of the Son, and of the Holy Spirit. Amen."

Some of the men were deeply moved by what Don had to say. Others thought it was just a con. He'd caused a lot of hurt in the past. Jeff Farmer wasn't yet a Christian, but he said to me later, "Jan, whether Don can live what he preached is yet to be proven, but I believe he sincerely meant every word he spoke at that moment. I'm willing to give him a chance."

Henry Dawson chose to step forward after Don. "I've been waiting a long time for this moment. I tried running my life my way, and it brought me to disaster. I'm giving over the running of myself to Jesus. He's my friend, and I know I can trust Him with my life."

Standing more than a foot taller than I, Henry had to stoop his six feet, two inch frame for me to pour the water over his head. "I baptize you, Henry, in the name of the Father, and of the Son, and of the Holy Spirit. Amen."

Cary Williams stepped forward. With tears running down his sweet, black face he said, "Dear Lord, I love you so much. Let this baptism symbolize to You my dedication to serve You for the rest of my life."

The inmate photographer took pictures and listened intently as each man came forward. I could see he was deeply moved.

Roberto "Castro" Miranda stepped forward and said in his broken English, "I never heard of Jesus until Jannie and Mitchie came to see me at jail. I know Jesus loves me because for four years I didn't have anyone. Only Sister Donitella to write to me. God sent me a family to love me. Before I had no faith or hope. Now I have Jesus and I am never alone."

Manuel Lopez is generally quiet and reserved, especially in a crowd. This day was no different. He simply said, "I love Jesus and I'd like to be baptized." No flowery speech was necessary.

Randy Moore brought tears to almost everyone's eyes as he said, "I served Satan when I was out on the streets. We all serve him in one way or another unless we consciously make a decision to serve Christ, but I chose to worship Satan. Today is Good Friday, the day Jesus gave

His life for each of us. It is the day I choose to publicly
and proudly give my life back to Him."

Ricky Sechrest is enormously shy and uncomfortable in
a crowd. I didn't know if he would be able to stand before
these men and speak, but he stepped boldly forward. I
was enormously proud of him. I was quite sure he was
shaking inside, but he never let it show. He said, "I want
to thank God for Mom and Dad and for allowing them to
come here to baptize us. Through them we can see how
much He loves each of us. I want to thank Charlie for
being here with me too. I gave my heart to Jesus in the jail
while I was waiting for trial. Now I want to be baptized as
a symbol of that promise to Him."

As Ricky sat down, his friend Charlie stood up and
came forward, much to everyone's surprise. Charlie said,
"I know I am just a visitor here today and I thank you for
allowing me the privilege of being with you. What you
have shared today has touched me so deeply that I would
like to be baptized too, if you will let me." And so it was,
Charlie was baptized along with the rest of our little
family.

I looked around the room. It contained both Christians
and non-believers. As my eyes scanned each face, they
locked on Jeff Farmer. As he squirmed in his chair I said,
"Jeff, are you ready to be baptized?" He grinned and
shook his head no. Jeff didn't believe God existed—or so
he said.

"Pete, how about you? Are you ready yet?" Pete's face
turned pink as he shook his snow white halo of hair and
said, "Not yet, maybe next time."

At six feet, four inches, Jimmy Neuschafer had a hard
time hiding from me, even though he was trying to be
inconspicuous. I walked up to him, placed my hands on
his shoulders and said, "Jimmy, isn't it about time?" To the
amazement of every one in the room, Jimmy ambled to the
front where Gary stood waiting and said, "Ya, it's time.

I've put God on the back burner long enough!" With that declaration Jimmy bent nearly in half so I could reach the top of his head to pour the water and baptize him.

Shortly after the baptisms ended, the guards came to claim their captives. Although everyone groaned and no one wanted the visit to end, I think each of us needed time alone, to reflect on what had happened that day. Of this Gary and I are certain, no one would walk away from that room unaffected!

After our return to Las Vegas, Randy Moore sent us an article he had written for the new issue of *The Rising Son*. Randy wrote:

Making the decision to be baptized was one of the most important decisions I've ever made. Not just for the obvious reasons, but because of my past involvement with witchcraft and the occult. Baptism is a serious matter to me. I believe it should be a conscious decision with a lot of thought for its meaning. Jesus instructed us to count the cost before we committed our lives to Him.

I guess I disagree with a lot of people on one thing concerning baptism. God gives us a choice to serve Him or Satan. Baptizing a baby who has no concept of what is going on, makes no sense to me. Where is the freedom of choice? Babies cannot exercise the free will God has given to us.

I was baptized April 16, 1987, shortly after my twenty-second birthday. I had to decide between the constant temptations of practicing witchcraft again or putting it all behind me and doing the very best I could to love and serve God. I didn't want to be baptized until I could make a commitment to Christ to serve Him with my whole heart, mind, and soul.

It was not only a commitment to God and to myself, but a way of trying to let God know I had made a decision to turn away from witchcraft and all its evils and

*serve Him to the best of my ability. It was a public
declaration of my love for Him. I want to be what He
wants me to be, and I want Him to guide my life in
whatever direction He wants.*

> *Jan and Gary came to the prison on Good Friday
and baptized eleven of us men. They made me feel
comfortable when I was nervous. Not because everyone
else was there, but because of how important the event was
in my life. It was even more special to me because they
were the ones to baptize me. Good Friday was the day
Jesus lay down His life so we could live, and it is the day
we publicly gave our lives back to him."*

It took a lot of courage for those men to stand before
their non-believing peers and take the stand they did. I
never think of April 16, 1987 without recalling Isaiah 49:16:
"...behold, I have inscribed you on the palms of My
hands!"

Many people doubt what they call "jail house
conversions." They have the idea the men and women in
prison use "religion" as a way out the back door. At times
there are some in prison who do use it as a con. They get
Christians from the community to write letters to the
parole board on their behalf and to help find them jobs.

Gary and I saw it happen with more than one man at
the medium security prison. However, there is nothing for
a death row inmate to gain by professing to be a Christian.
He or she never goes before a parole board, and the courts
want to hear "case law" and hard facts.

Before we left that day the young inmate photographer
who had been with us all day approached Gary and me
and said, "I wish I would have had the courage to speak up
while I was in there with you, like Charlie did. For the
first time in my life I realized today, there is a God and He
loves me. I saw His love written on every face in that

room. The next time you come back, do you think you guys could baptize me?"

Our only regret is that we didn't have a chance to baptize that young man before we left. All the men on death row were moved to a new super-maximum security prison 250 miles away before we had the funds to return. Our consolation is in knowing a seed was planted in his heart. He's serving a life sentence, but I pray that the Lord will send someone special to minister to him.

Several weeks after our visit, Pete Deutscher wrote his first article for *The Rising Son*. Gary and I were surprised because Pete is such a private person. I asked him if he wanted me to withhold his name and address, but he said, "No, print it, I'm proud that I wrote it and I don't care who knows."

Pete received several letters and made new friends because of this article:

FRIENDS CAME TO SEE ME

I had been on death row for nine years before I received my first religious visit. On Christmas day, 1986 I got to meet the people who had sent me and every other person on our death row a Christmas card one year earlier. On the card they wrote a short note saying they were friends of Henry Dawson, another inmate on our row. They said they would like to visit with me when they came to the prison.

I said to myself, "This new guy has been giving my name to some Jesus freaks and now they want to come and see me." I found out later they wanted to see each of us. Well, if everyone was going, I wasn't staying in the unit by myself. I was going too.

The day they came everyone in the unit was shaving, showering, and putting on their best clothes. I did the same thing. I wasn't going to let anyone outdo

me. That visit was one to remember. Jan and Gary gave
all of us a big hug and a big smile to go with it. I would
bet their were twenty guys from death row in the visiting
room that day—all at one time. That has never happened
before. The guards were nice and friendly. I thought I
was dreaming.

They came for a second visit three months later,
for Easter. Ricky Sechrest, another guy from the row, had
a visit with a friend named Charlie. Charlie wasn't with
Jan and Gary, but he saw the good that was being done
and jumped right into visiting all of us. In fact, after the
visit Charlie gave them a bouquet of flowers and signed it
from all of us guys on the row.

These people were here to talk about God, but they
didn't discuss any particular religion. I also met the guy
named Henry Dawson, who lived in a different unit.
That little woman took charge of us guys and lit a fire
under us all. As the day came to an end, everyone was
thankful they had come.

The second day when I was called, I was ready in
minutes. This time after we collected our hugs, we were
ushered into a room just to the side of the regular visiting
room. Eight men had requested to be baptized and Jan
and Gary got permission from the Governor to come and
baptize them. After the others were baptized, Jan pulled
me off to the side and asked me if I wanted to be baptized
with them.

I wanted to tell her yes because Gary and her had
been so nice to me and I didn't want to hurt their feelings,
but I knew that wasn't the right reason for me to say yes.
I stalled by saying, "The next time you come I'll be first
in line."

Since those two days, when the Rising Son
Ministry came into my life, a lot of people have been
writing to me. I've never written so many letters in my
life as I have since I met Jan and Gary Hoffman.

The last four years on the row have been filled with loving and caring. Just the joy of knowing these people is good for me. What do you call people who can keep your mind off of death row? They have even given me their phone number and said I can call if I need to talk. Now, some people I've known for years have never made me that offer—nor have they come to visit me for that matter.

That night after everyone was locked up, I looked at my Living Bible that Jan and Gary had sent me and I said to myself, "these people have kept me busy thinking about the Lord for the past two years and I didn't even know it." I looked up faith in my Bible. "What is faith?" I wondered. Hebrews 11:1 says, "What is faith, it is the confident assurance that something we want is going to happen. It is the certainty that what we hope for is waiting for us, even though we cannot see it up ahead." I had it all the time, I just didn't know it. Jan and Gary, I'm ready to be baptized.

I pray that none of you brothers and sisters on death row ever give up hope. Ultimately, the Lord is all we have.

CHAPTER SEVEN
The Third Generation

" *Even so it is not the will of your Father which is in heaven, that one of these little ones should perish.*"

Matthew 18:14, KJV

When we made our first contact with the prisoners on Nevada's death row, after the execution of Carroll Edward Cole on December 6, 1985, the first response letter we received was from Gerald Gallego Junior. We didn't know why he was condemned to die and we didn't ask. We simply offered our friendship and let him know we didn't expect anything in return. Gerald accepted our friendship and after several years of corresponding with him, we found out that Gerald represents the third generation of his family who will die in prison.

His grandfather, Pablo Gallego, died of natural causes while incarcerated for theft in California's notorious San Quentin Prison. Pablo and his wife, Daisy, had four children. Because Daisy was poor and her children too young to claim the body, Pablo was buried in the old prison cemetery.

Gerald's father, Gerald Gallego Senior, was executed on March 3, 1955. He was the first person to die in Mississippi's gas chamber. He was sentenced to death for the murder of a policeman.

Today, Gerald Junior sits on Nevada's death row awaiting execution. In his entire life, he never met his father.

In response to our Christmas card, Gerald wrote that he wasn't a Christian and wasn't interested in becoming one. We wrote back and said, "Gerald, it doesn't matter to us that you aren't a Christian. We are still offering our hands in friendship. The Lord is an important part of our lives, and we will probably talk about him from time to time, but we won't preach."

In the months that followed, we shared many letters with Gerald and he became a special friend. By now we were pen pals to over twenty-one prisoners on Nevada's death row.

We fretted over the letters we received from Gerald. Of all the men and women we were writing to, Gerald seemed to be the most depressed. We tried to write cheerful tidbits to lift his spirits, but depression continued to cling to him. We ended our letters with "God bless you" or "We pray for you," but we never tried to push Gerald into accepting something he didn't believe in. Not only was he not sure Jesus was the Son of God, he wasn't even sure that God existed.

After several months of corresponding with Gerald, I wrote him a letter that started out with my normal cheerful chatter. As the letter progressed, I found myself sharing a Bible story with him. I attempted to explain why I had become a Christian and used the story as an illustration. After I mailed the letter, I worried that I may have offended him. After all, I had promised I would not preach to him and I was concerned that he might interpret it that way. The following day I wrote him a note and apologized.

In Gerald's response letter he said, "Jan, let me explain something to you. Every year around Christmas time I receive a letter from a minister in California. It starts off, 'Dear Gerald,' and then there are six or seven pages of Bible verses. Let me ask you a question, is he doing this for me or himself? You are my friend. You care that I am lonesome, and you care because I am worried about the welfare of my little boy. You are my friend and because you care, you can say anything you want to say."

This was a turning point in our friendship. I no longer felt restrained when I wrote to Gerald. I never preached, but when I thought an illustration from the Bible was appropriate, I shared it.

The main source of Gerald's depression was caused by two things. His wife, Charlene, had testified against him in court and hurt him deeply, yet he was still in love with her. Gerald was also greatly distressed because he could not see his son. Gerald never knew his father, and lives with the fear that his son will never know him.

The only people who Gerald trusted enough to correspond with were his mother, his attorney, and Gary and me. Although Gerald would write to his mother, he only received one letter from her. "She promised to visit me," Gerald said, "but she never did. I hoped she would, but I knew in my heart that she wouldn't. My philosophy is, I hope for the best, but expect the worst." When his mother committed suicide, Gerald was devastated.

He stopped writing to us for over a year. Although he never said it, I believe he was afraid to allow himself to get too attached to us for fear God would take us away from him. On the few occasions that Gerald opened up and talked about God, it seemed to me that he was under the impression that God's wrath was upon him.

I continued to write to Gerald. Even though he didn't write back, I felt sure he read the letters I sent to him. I reasoned that if he didn't want to read them, he would have written, "Return to Sender" on the envelope and sent them back.

Gerald finally broke his year of silence. The first sentence of his letter said, "Boy, you just don't give up do you?" I smiled and thought, "Welcome home, Gerald."

I got to meet Gerald on our second visit to the prison. He was wearing an orange jumpsuit, which only the highest security risk prisoners were required to wear. His legs were shackled and one wrist was cuffed to his belly chain.

We were separated by thick bulletproof glass, and in addition there were bars on my side. There was no phone, so we had to yell to hear each other. The visiting area on each side of the glass partition was no larger than an average bathroom. It was evident that Gerald was nervous, and he spent most of the forty-five-minute visit talking about his son. Other than occasional seeing his attorney, this was Gerald's first visit in five years.

Gerald felt bitterness towards his mother because of her refusal to tell him the truth about his father. No matter what the truth was about him, Gerald felt he had a right to know. He also resented the fact that his father had looked for him when he was a baby, but his mother wouldn't allow a visit. The Senior Gallego was executed, not knowing whether the child he fathered was a boy or a girl. Gerald is determined that his son will know him, so he decided to write his memoirs. I have promised to hold this journal for safe keeping and deliver it to his son when he is eighteen.

As Gerald sent me sections of his journal, I began to understand why he doesn't believe that there is a loving heavenly Father. The abuse he suffered as a child at the hands of his stepfather is almost inconceivable to me. His mother, Lorraine, made little effort to put a stop to it.

Before Lorraine met George Bulgar she was alone with a nineteen-month-old son and pregnant with Gerald. Her husband, Gerald Albert Gallego, had been arrested for auto theft and for writing bad checks and was sent to San Quentin Prison. She had no place to stay and no one to help her. When Lorraine met George, it seemed like an answer to her prayers. She moved in with him and divorced her husband. Lorraine and George Bulgar were married a short time later. This was George's first marriage.

George and his father co-owned a bar called the Lion's Den. He was a cruel man by nature, but when he drank his cruelty was magnified. Night after night Lorraine would cover her ears as her two son's screams pierced the darkness of the bedroom which she shared with George. She did not dare rush to her children's defense, for fear of the beating she herself would certainly receive. She did nothing.

In the next room Lorraine's sons, David and Gerald, cowered under their blankets for fear their drunken stepfather would burn their hands again with his cigar.

Each night Gerald struggled to stay awake as long as he could, crying, trembling, and wondering if George would come to his room. Some nights he did and some nights he didn't, but Gerald cried every night.

In the beginning, Gerald tried to show George that he cared for him, hoping it would make a difference. It didn't.

When Gerald was six years old, his stepfather urinated in a glass and made him drink it. George would beat the boys with his fists and with broom handles. He would make them stand with their hands in the air and their faces turned to the kitchen wall while he ate breakfast. Gerald's arms would ache and burn in their raised position, but he didn't dare lower them or protest. Because of Lorraine's passive character, George had total control over her and the children and he used this power every day.

One night as seven-year-old Gerald waited in his bed for George to come home, he decided to kill him. The next morning before George came to the kitchen for breakfast, Gerald poured ant poison into his coffee. George tasted it and immediately spit it out. He thought Lorraine had put it in his coffee and beat her.

Gerald ran out of the house and hid in the back yard. As his mother's screams went on and on, he desperately wanted to return to the house and tell his stepfather that he had done it, but he was afraid. His courage died with the beating of his mother and Gerald never tried such an attempt again.

Gerald knew he wasn't a Bulgar—he was a Gallego. "Jan," Gerald commented, "I used to lay in bed and fervently pray that my father would come and rescue me from this nightmare. I dreamed that we would go away, father and son, and life would be good. My prayers went unanswered, the dream never materialized, and the loving father I so longed for never came to rescue me." The nightmare he was living continued.

"Gerald, you had a father who couldn't love you, a stepfather who didn't love you, and a Heavenly Father who wants to love you. He is waiting for you to crawl up on his lap. Won't you just give Him a chance?" I pleaded.

Shortly after Gerald attempted to poison his stepfather, he was arrested for running away and was returned home, where a severe punishment awaited him—a pattern which was to be repeated over and over again.

I asked Gerald why his mother didn't leave George Bulgar. He responded, "I asked her that once after he had beaten me. She told me that as long as she stayed with him, we would at least have food on the table and a roof over our heads." This was of little consolation to Gerald.

At age nine, Gerald's dream of his father rescuing him died when he inadvertently learned that his father was on death row in Mississippi. When Gerald confronted his mother, she lied and told him his father had been killed in 1946, during the war. "I suspected my mother was lying," Gerald commented, "but either way, I knew my father would not come."

George Bulgar was forced out of business and arrested for income tax evasion. He served six months in prison.

With no money for groceries, Gerald and his brother David went door to door, looking for odd jobs. Although they occasionally got lucky and were able to make a few dollars cutting grass, it was never enough. They began stealing food from grocery stores and from neighbor's homes. "My mother never asked us where the food came from," Gerald commented, "but I think she knew."

George returned home from his prison stint with a vengeance and the beatings began in earnest. Gerald's flights from home became more frequent and he continued stealing—so he could stay away longer. Gerald developed a love/hate relationship with his mother. He loved her because she was his mother, but hated her for her refusal to even make a token attempt to defend him or David from the abuse his stepfather so liberally inflicted upon them.

Lorraine gave birth to two more children after her marriage to George Bulgar. By the age of ten, George Jr. had lost eighty percent of the hearing in one ear and forty percent of his hearing in the other, from blows he received to the head. Even George Bulgar's own children were not spared his wrath.

"By the age of eleven, I was completely out of control, Gerald said, "I would run away from home, steal to survive, and be arrested by the police and returned to my mother." Not one person ever intervened on behalf of the abused child. At age twelve Gerald entered the juvenile court system and through age twenty-one was arrested for a number of crimes including arson, auto theft, and assault with a deadly weapon. When Gerald was released from Paso Robles School for Boys at age thirteen, he reentered the mainstream of public school. One day when Gerald returned home from class, his stepfather made a threatening move on him and something inside of Gerald snapped. "I beat George until he was down on the floor and bloody. My stepfather never beat me again. After that incident I came and went as I pleased, but I never had to run away from home again. My stepfather and I simply avoided each other as much as possible."

"I hated school," Gerald told me, "not for the same reasons as most boys, but because of the ridicule I received when I did attend. There was never money to provide nice clothing nor was there money for lunch. My favorite class was Physical Education, but even to attend PE I had to steal tennis shoes, a jock strap, and shorts out of someone's locker. Because I didn't have money, when the lunch bell rang, I would hide in the alley until it was time to return to class." Gerald dropped out of school in the eleventh grade.

At the age of twenty-three, Gerald was convicted of armed robbery and received a five to life sentence. When he was released from prison at the age of twenty-seven, he was determined to make a change. His robbing and stealing days were over.

Gerald didn't have any trouble obtaining a job. He was a good looking young man with hazel eyes, well-groomed wavy brown hair and a cheerful smile that revealed even white teeth. Gerald's wide shoulders and trim waist were nicely proportioned for his five feet, nine inch frame.

Gerald went to work at the Del Mar Club as a bartender. He loved his job and likened it to being at a party and getting paid for it. After changing jobs several times, Gerald ended up at the Chico Club. Not only did the club have a live band and a dance floor, but it also had a card room where lo-ball poker was played.

Two men who Gerald had become friends with operated the card room. One night they had a fight and split up the partnership. Gerald was taken in as a partner to replace the one who left. The game was a gold mine and Gerald made five times what he earned as a bartender. Eventually Gerald opened his own card room.

Gerald's best friend at that time was Lonnie David, a man he had known since childhood. Lonnie was in love with a woman named Bonnie and wanted to settle down and get married. He wanted Gerald to double date with him and Bonnie, but Gerald told him that he ran the card room all night, slept all day, and didn't know any women.

The next night, Lonnie returned to the card room and called Gerald out of the game. "Gerald, I'd like you to meet my girlfriend Bonnie and this is her friend, Charlene Williams."

He knew that Lonnie was going to try to line him up with a blind date and had tried everything he could think of to get out of it. Now he couldn't take his eyes off of the green-eyed blond. Here sat the girl of his dreams.

Gerald reluctantly returned to the card game and tried everything in his power to break the game up so he could spend the evening with Charlene, but the game didn't break up until 4:30 in the morning. Bonnie and Lonnie had left much earlier, but Charlene waited at a small table for Gerald to finish. After driving her home, Gerald walked her to the door and kissed her good night. Gerald and Charlene began seeing each other every day. Within two weeks Gerald moved in with her and one year later they drove to Reno and got married.

"Jan," Gerald said, "the good times Charlene and I shared together were so good, but the bad times were so bad. She was like no one I had ever met before. She didn't need a man in the way most women need a man. I couldn't understand why she wanted to be with me. It wasn't love, it wasn't sex, and it certainly wasn't my money. Charlene's family was quite comfortable, financially. She was intelligent, cunning, devious, and manipulative. I knew all of these things, and yet I didn't care. I didn't understand why she wanted to be with me, but I was so in love with her that the reasons didn't matter—we were together."

Charlene was consumed with jealousy even though Gerald gave her no reason to be. She would fly into a rage when Gerald had friends over for a visit. Finally Gerald asked them not to come anymore. She insisted that Gerald give up his card room and go to work for her father. When he resisted, Charlene hinted that she would leave him, so Gerald began driving a truck for her father. "Jan, I hated every minute of it," Gerald told me, "but I would have done whatever it took to keep her happy. I lived in fear that I would lose Charlene, and my fear gave her power."

She began passing bad checks all over town and Gerald spent a fortune trying to cover them. He was afraid she would go to jail and he would do anything to protect her.

On November 17, 1980, Gerald and Charlene were arrested by the FBI on a California warrant charging them each with two counts of murder. On July 28, 1981, Charlene and her attorney tried to make a deal with the Sacramento district attorney's office. She signed a contract stating that if the district attorney used her testimony to convict Gerald that all charges would be dropped against her, but after five hours of intense questioning the district attorney said no deal. He didn't believe her story and he filed notice with the court that he intended to seek the death penalty against both her and Gerald.

Charlene changed attorneys in March, 1982. Once again Charlene and her attorney approached the district attorney, only this time she claimed their were eight murders committed, instead of the two her and Gerald were charged with. Two of these murders took place in Nevada.

Charlene turned state's evidence and worked out a plea bargain agreement with the district attorney in which she agreed to testify against Gerald. All charges were dropped against her in California and she received a sixteen-year sentence in Nevada. The agreement was that she would serve the full sixteen year sentence, with no time off for good behavior.

Charlene was seven months pregnant at the time of their arrest. She gave birth to a son on January 17, 1981.

Gerald was given the death penalty in California and in Nevada. The news media dubbed him a sex slave serial murderer. He is called this because of Charlene's testimony against him. While on the witness stand, she claimed her husband was looking for the perfect sex slave.

According to Charlene, she would drive the van and scout for pretty young women to help satisfy Gerald's hearty sexual appetite. She claimed she would lure these young woman to the van and drive around while her husband sexually assaulted and then murdered them. Her testimony was so convincing that the jury sentenced Gerald to death.

Gerald has maintained throughout our eight-year friendship that he is innocent of these murders. He said Charlene had many lesbian affairs, but he was so in love with her that he turned a blind eye to them. Gerald told us he had proof that he was not in Nevada when the murders took place because he has pay stubs that proved he was working in California. This information was presented to the jury, but they apparently believed Charlene's testimony was stronger. Although there was evidence to link Charlene to the murders, there was no physical evidence to link Gerald to the crimes. It was Charlene's testimony alone that convicted him.

We have grown to care for Gerald, and at first it was difficult for us to believe that he is innocent, however, we have never known him to lie to us about anything. I guess it is somehow easier to believe a man is guilty of these horrible crimes than it is to believe a woman is guilty. The truth is, it doesn't matter to us whether he is guilty or innocent. If he is innocent, there is nothing we can do to help him, and if he is guilty, we still care about him.

On May 12, 1991, the *Reno Gazette-Journal* ran a three page story on Charlene. The headline on the front page read: "Did the Wife Get Away with Murder?" The headlines over the articles inside read: "Wife's Role in Murders Questioned," and "Did Gallego Receive a Fair Trial?"

After serving just ten years of her sentence, the state of Nevada wants to release Charlene because she has earned good time credit—but according to the plea agreement, she must serve the whole sixteen-year sentence.

The lead article stated that Charlene had engaged in a number of lesbian affairs before and after she went to prison, although none of this came out in court. The detective who helped prosecute Gerald was quoted as saying, "Her style was to pull the strings subtly, behind the scenes. She would discover a man's weak points and use them to her advantage." He also stated that she is "cunning and manipulative."

A Reno attorney who did some legal research on the case was quoted as saying, "She is a conniving woman who got caught. She had to come up with a story or face the death penalty. To believe the case, you have to believe her. And she is the weirdest character in the whole story."

I sent the article to Gerald. I thought after all the bad press he has received for the past ten years that he would be overjoyed that someone was finally questioning Charlene's culpability. Everything Gerald had been telling us was written on the pages of that newspaper.

I said, "Gerald, surely someone will investigate this now."

With a heavy heart Gerald responded, "Jan if you will notice, some of the people that put me on death row were quoted in the paper. They have known about this right from the start and did nothing. I don't expect them to do anything now."

Gerald fears for his son's safety if she is released. He said, "If Charlene serves her full sentence, my son will be sixteen years old and by that time he will be his own man. If she is released now, she can manipulate him because he is still pliable."

I asked Gerald if he thought she would still present a danger to the community. Gerald paused for several minutes and with tears in his voice he said, "I'm afraid of it, Jan."

We continue to minister to Gerald and try to show him how loving our Heavenly Father is, but Gerald still isn't convinced. He said, "Jan, if there is a God, we haven't met. It isn't that I don't want to believe in God—God doesn't want to believe in me!"

Gerald wants a sign, something to show him that God is indeed a loving Father who cares for His children. The only prototype of a kind and loving father that Gerald has to draw from is his childhood dream of his father rescuing him. Gerald is forty-four years old and has never been loved just for himself.

Perhaps one day Gerald will realize that it is God who sent Gary and I to love him. If there was a verse in the Bible I could claim for Gerald it would be Psalms 27:10-14: "For if my mother and father should abandoned me, you would welcome and comfort me. Tell me what to do, oh Lord, and make it plain because I am surrounded by waiting enemies. Don't let them get me, Lord! Don't let me fall into their hands! For they accuse me of things I never did, and all the while are plotting cruelty. I am expecting the Lord to rescue me again, so that once again I will see His goodness to me here in the land of the living. Don't be impatient. Wait for the Lord, and He will come and save you! Be brave, stouthearted, and courageous. Yes, wait and He will help you."

CHAPTER EIGHT
"Oh Yes, Mama, I'm Sure"

"You have heard that it was said, 'Love your neighbor and hate your enemy.' But I tell you: Love your enemies and pray for those who persecute you, that you may be sons of your Father in heaven."

Matthew 5:43-45

"If you don't give me the death penalty I'll kill guards, I'll kill homosexuals, and I'll kill other inmates," the voice blared as I stepped into the living room to watch the nightly news. Approaching the television set, I saw an angry young man sporting a goatee and a shaved head, issuing an ultimatum to the judge he stood before.

Sean Flanagan had given up his right to a jury trial and asked to go before a three-judge panel. His cocky demeanor and boastful threats were certain to gain him disfavor with the judges. If he kept it up he was destined to get his wish. He stood before the toughest judge in the district court.

Later that evening as I sat in my den answering a stack of letters, impulsively I reached into the desk drawer and pulled out three copies of *The Rising Son*. Before dropping them in a large envelope I stuck a large yellow post-it note on the front of one which read: "Dear Sean, We don't necessarily agree with what you are doing, but we want you to know we care. If you need a friend, give us a call. Love in Christ, Gary and Jan Hoffman."

This was February 1988. Two weeks later as Gary and I were driving to work I heard a radio announcer say, "Sean Patrick Flanagan was sentenced to death yesterday by a three-judge panel for the murder of a homosexual who made sexual advances toward him. A second trial is scheduled in two weeks for the murder of a second homosexual who also made advances toward him. He will appear before the same three-judge panel. Mr. Flanagan is also asking the state to give him the ultimate penalty in that case, death by lethal injection."

Three hours after Gary and I opened our store, the phone rang on the ministry line. "Good morning, Rising Son Ministry," I greeted. A breathless young voice on the other end said in a rush, "I've only got a minute until they lock me back in my cell. My name is Sean Flanagan. You sent me those newsletters and the note. You said if I needed a friend, I could call you. I just accepted Jesus as my Savior and I have so many questions to ask. Can you come to see me?" I promised Sean I'd be there later that evening.

Gary had an appointment but he encouraged me to go see Sean. As I sat at the window in the visiting room, I saw the guards escorting a cute, red-haired, freckle-faced young man in full body chains. I knew he was being held in the hole for fighting or some major infraction of rules. Only inmates from the hole were left in chains for a visit. The guard released the handcuff from his right hand so he could hold the phone to his ear, but his other hand was left chained to his side and his feet were shackled in chains.

As Sean took a seat on his side of the glass window, he positively glowed. His hair had started to grow back and he had shaved off the goatee. If someone had told me this is the same man I saw on TV two weeks earlier, I wouldn't have believed it.

"Sean, tell me what happened." I said, "You told me you have accepted the Lord!"

Sean looked thoughtful and said, "I was so happy the day the judge told me I got the death penalty. That is what I wanted. That night when I went to bed I thought, "When I am executed, will I go to heaven or hell?" I honestly didn't know. I called for the chaplain and Chaplain Bonnie came to see me. She explained the plan of salvation and said if I would repent Jesus would forgive me. I laid in bed all night thinking about what she said. The next morning a preacher named Ted came to see me and asked me if I was ready to make a commitment to the Lord. I said yes, and we prayed together."

After a pause he added, "I want to ask some questions, Jan, but please don't laugh at me. Keep in mind that until yesterday, all I knew about Jesus was that His name was a swear word." I assured him I wouldn't laugh.

"Before you begin, Sean," I said, "I don't want to misrepresent myself. I am not an ordained minister. I may not have all the answers, but if I am unsure, I will tell you so, and I'll talk to my pastor and get the correct answer for you. I read my Bible every day. I've read it through twice, and I know the overall message God has given us, but I am by no means an authority."

His first question came as a total surprise to me. I don't know what I expected, but it wasn't this question. I didn't laugh, but I had to smile because, in retrospect, if I knew nothing about the Bible it would be a question I would have been likely to ask.

"Jan, where did the devil come from?" Sean asked with a serious look on his face.

"Satan," I explained, "was an angel and he was God's most perfect and beautiful creation. He allowed himself to get puffed up with pride and wanted to be worshiped like God. There was a war in heaven and Satan was cast to earth, along with the angels who worshiped him." I went on to explain the story of the Garden of Eden.

Sean looked puzzled and said, "You mean because Adam and Eve sinned, everyone else who is ever born is also a sinner?"

I said, "Well, Sean, let me explain this way. Now this is my own personal opinion. The first thing that happened when Adam and Eve disobeyed God was they noticed they were naked. They had walked and talked with God, and they never noticed they were naked before. God's intent when He created man was that we should keep our eyes on Him. When Adam and Eve sinned, they took their eyes off God and turned them on themselves. It is when we turn to Jesus and ask Him to forgive us, that we turn our eyes away from self and return them back to God, where they should have stayed. When you consider the sin of pride next to murder, it doesn't seem like a very big deal, and yet that is the very reason Satan was thrown out of heaven. Pride keeps many people from turning their lives over to Jesus."

Sean asked a second question, "How does God feel about the death penalty?"

"Well Sean," I said thoughtfully, "as far as I can tell, it's not a black and white issue. Christians can make a case either way based on the Bible. I happen to oppose capital punishment, although at one time I believed in it. I oppose it for two reasons now. First, I saw how unfairly it was meted out in our friend Henry Dawson's case, and other cases we've followed since. Second, when the Jewish leaders tossed an adulteress at Jesus' feet and said, 'This woman was caught in the act of adultery. According to the law of Moses she is to be stoned to death. What do you say?' Now Sean, they were trying to trap Jesus because, according to Roman law, the Jews weren't allowed to administer capital punishment. Jesus said, 'If any of you is without sin, let him be the first to throw a stone at her'(John 8:3-11). With that He bent and started to write in the dirt. When He stood, everyone was gone. He looked at the adulteress and said, 'Has no one accused you?' She said, 'No sir, not one.'

Jesus said, 'Then neither do I. Go and sin no more!' In one sense, Sean, Jesus was asked for His approval of capital punishment, and He didn't give it."

Changing the subject, Sean inquired, "Do you know how to sing, Jan?" I said, "Well, I'm no Amy Grant but I can carry a tune. Why do you ask?"

He said, "I only know one verse of 'Amazing Grace,' but I'd like to sing it with you." I looked around to see who might be listening and realized we were all alone on both sides of the glass, with the exception of the guard. He was on Sean's side and I didn't care if he heard Sean sing.

Having no vibrato in my voice and Sean's being slightly off key, I was relieved no one was there to hear us. I was embarrassed as we began, but as the first chords filled the air, Sean and I thought we sounded like angels. We sang the first verse twice and followed it with repetitions of "Praise God." It was a special moment for both of us.

When we finished, Sean again asked what the Bible had to say about the death penalty. I responded, "Well, Exodus 21:23 says, '...A life for a life, an eye for an eye, a tooth for a tooth...' But in Matthew 5:38 Jesus said, 'You have heard it said, An eye for an eye, and a tooth for a tooth, but I tell you, do not resist an evil person. If someone strikes you on the right cheek turn to him the other also.'

"There is another verse in Ezekiel 33:11 that says, 'As sure as I live declares the Sovereign Lord, I delight not in the death of the wicked but would rather that they turn from their evil ways and live.' Sean, Christ's death on the cross covered all sin, not just some sin. To God sin is sin.

When we ask Jesus to forgive us, it's like our sins are all listed on a big chalk board and Jesus erases every trace with an eraser. God's Word says, 'For as high as the heavens are above the earth, so great is his love for those who fear him; as far as the east is from the west, so far will our transgressions be removed from us' (Psalms 103:12)."

That seemed to satisfy Sean, and he asked what Nevada's death row was like. I told him about our two visits and shared a little about our "family" there.

A third time Sean asked about the death penalty. "Sean," I said, finally understanding, "are you worried about what you did to deliberately get the death sentence?" With big tears in his eyes he nodded yes.

Gently I said, "Oh Sean, were you a Christian when you went through all those courtroom antics?" He shook his head no and said, "I didn't even know who Jesus was then, Jan."

"Sean, this is an allegory of what I think happens when we give our life to Jesus." I shared with him a story I wrote for the first issue of *The Rising Son*:

> *The moment you invite Jesus into your heart you are instantly transported to heaven and placed at the feet of God. He says to you, "My child, you now belong to me. You are a child of heaven for all time and eternity. I love you, You are Mine, but I need your help. I need you to go back to earth for a short while. You see there are other people I want saved, just as I wanted you saved. No one will be able to touch their hearts the way you can, my child. You can save them from the choke-hold Satan has on them. It won't be easy for you, my child. Satan will be angry at you for doing My work. He will use all the powers of hell to win your soul back from Me. He will hit your weak spots hard, so be prepared, for he surely knows what they are!*

"Trust Me, my child, I will not allow you to be tempted beyond what you can bear. My Son will help you. Keep your eyes on Him. He loves you so much that had you been the only person on earth, He would have died on the cross just for you. Jesus will never fail you, never!

"Your time on earth may seem long, but compared to eternity it is just a blink of the eye. Satan may whisper lies in your ear and tell you I have abandoned you—that I don't love you. Don't listen to him, he is the world's master liar! I am here, I love you, you are Mine!

"Give Me all your worries and your cares. I will tenderly guard over everything that concerns you. Earth is just a temporary labor field for you. You are there to do My will until I send Jesus to take your hand and bring you home to Me. For this moment remember that I sometimes allow you to have a tear in your eye... So I can put a rainbow in your heart!"

"Sean, I shared that story with you to show that God wants to use you. This jail and the prison are filled with people who are going to hell. Let God worry about when you are to die. For whatever time you have left, your job is to lead lost souls home. Some will listen and some won't, your job is to try."

"But, Jan," Sean protested, "how can God use me? I'm locked in my cell twenty-three hours a day. I'm willing, but I just don't see how God can use me."

"That's all He asks, Sean," I said, "for us to have a willing heart. Why not pray and ask the Lord to bring people to you?" With a smile Sean nodded and said he would.

The next day Sean called and was frantic. I could hear the tears in his voice as he said, "Jan, my attorney just told me that I can't go to heaven because God won't forgive a murderer. Is that true?"

"Hang in there, Sean," I muttered through gritted teeth, "I'll be right there." I quickly explained to Gary, grabbed my Bible, and headed for the jail.

Sean was still teary as he stepped to the window and picked up the phone. "What's this all about?" I gently asked as I tried to soothe him.

"Well," Sean said with a quiver in his voice, "my attorney came to see me today. I told him I had repented of my sins and he told me God doesn't forgive murderers. He said if you steal something you have to pay it back—make atonement, but if you take a life, you can't pay it back, so you can't be forgiven. Jan, is that true? Won't God forgive me?" A tear rolled down his cheek as he searched my face.

Opening my Bible to Luke 23:34, I pressed the page to the window and said, "Sean, what does that say? Read it for me."

"Father, forgive them, for they know not what they do." Sean's questioning look told me he didn't understand.

"Sean, those are words that Jesus spoke as he was hanging on the cross. He looked down at the people who were taking His life, the sinless Son of God, and asked His Father to forgive them. Don't you see, if Jesus could forgive His own murderers, He won't have any problem forgiving Sean Patrick Flanagan!" I could see relief wash over Sean as realization set in.

Learning his attorney's religion, I explained, "They believe in blood atonement; if you spill blood, you have to shed your own blood. Sean, the problem I have with that doctrine is the following: Why did Jesus have to go to the cross if we can make our own atonement? That makes His death senseless. Only Jesus could be the perfect sacrifice. He was the unblemished Lamb of God who takes away the sins of the world."

Like a dam that broke and spilled over, Sean began sharing his tragic childhood with me. "I was taken away from my mother when I was two years old because my baby brother died of malnutrition. I was near death myself because of lack of proper nourishment. The courts gave my sister and me to my father and stepmother. My stepmother had six children, and I never really fit into the family. My father was always abusive toward me. I don't think he really wanted me.

"My older brothers began sexually abusing me when I was only three or four years old. I lived in a nest of incest. Brothers with brothers, brothers with sisters, sisters with sisters and all of us together in one big orgy. I was so young I didn't know any better. I came to believe that was just the way families lived.

"One time my father and stepmother got into a fight, and my stepmother packed all the kids in the back of the pickup truck. I crawled into the back end, but she stopped the truck when she spied me and pushed me out onto the dirt road and said, 'Get out of here—you don't belong to us.' With those angry words she drove away and left me standing in the middle of the road, crying. I thought she was my mother. That incident broke my heart. I was only three years old, but I still remember the pain I felt.

"My father and stepmother patched up their relationship, but from that point on I knew I didn't really belong. When I was old enough, I joined the United States Marines. I was desperate to get away from my family. By then I knew what was going on with my siblings was wrong. I didn't recognize it as sin, because I didn't know what sin meant, but I knew it was sick. I had relationships with many women, but I also had two homosexual affairs.

"My whole life has been sick and depraved, Jan. I never knew a mother's or a father's love. I never had a healthy relationship with anyone. Would you mind if I call you Mother? I have a new Father who loves me for me—really loves me, and I know you love me too. Would you be my mama?" I was so choked up at his words, I could only nod.

Ted, the minister who led Sean to the Lord, continued to visit him twice a week to hold Bible studies. Ted is a mighty man of God, and Sean drew knowledge from Ted's teachings like a dry sponge soaking up living water. Gary and I continued to visit him twice a week. We affirmed Ted's teachings and acted as a source of support and comfort to Sean.

On one visit Sean told Gary and I about a Christian guard who worked on the graveyard shift. Every night the officer would go to Sean's cell when he wasn't busy with other responsibilities, and talk to him. Sean changed his sleeping habits so he would be awake when the guard came on duty. His deep caring had a profound effect on Sean.

Gary and I had an opportunity to meet this officer several months later, and we could understand Sean's love for him. What a striking contrast between him and the guard who taunts Frank Rodriguez. A Christian guard has a tremendous opportunity for ministry and we were privileged to see the fruit of the guard's labor.

When Sean went back for his second trial before the three-judge panel, he asked me if I would go to court with him. He was scared to death. "Mama," Sean said, "How am I going to explain to those judges I have changed my mind, and I don't want the death penalty? I've been begging them for months to execute me and now that I have changed my mind, what do I tell them? I don't mind if I look like a fool, but I don't want to make God look foolish."

Brushing the tears from my eyes with my finger tips, I said, "Sean, I promise you, God is a big enough God to handle whatever heat is put on Him because of this situation."

In the days Sean waited to go back before the three judges, God answered his daily prayers. Each day he asked God to use him to bring someone for him to minister to. From his isolation cell in the hole, Sean led six men to the Lord. Two were scheduled for extradition back to their states. Sean asked me to meet with them before they left.

I first met with Roy who had broken his girlfriend and himself out of jail in Kentucky. Together they went on a cross-country crime spree. Roy explained that he had once known the Lord, but had blown it and gone back to living for the world. Sean spent hours talking to him and encouraged him to rededicate his life to Christ. Roy knew he was facing at least one life sentence when he was returned to Kentucky. He decided he would spend the rest of his life serving Christ.

Roy's primary concern for the moment was for his girlfriend who was in the women's unit of the jail. Her pregnancy was almost full term. He was concerned for her health and the health of her soul. "Jan," Roy said earnestly, "Teresa doesn't know that I was once a Christian. I never told her, and my life since I met her certainly hasn't reflected holy living. It is important to me that she know the Lord. Will you go to her and tell her I have given my life back to Jesus, and show her the way to the Lord?"

I only met with Teresa once because she was extradited the next day, but she prayed the sinner's prayer with me before I left that night. Teresa was sentenced to five years, and Roy is serving a life sentence at the Kentucky State Prison. Both are doing time with Jesus.

Roy started a powerful ministry with the men on the yard. He was known as a tough guy when he served time at the same prison in previous years. He was looked up to and respected; no one messed with him. It took a lot of courage for him to go back on that same yard—with a Bible under his arm. Satan fights him every step of the way, but is losing ground.

The second man Sean asked me to see was Bill. Bill had so much to say during the visit that I hardly said a word. I recognized his need to talk and remained silent. "I owe Sean my life," Bill began, "I tried to commit suicide. That's why I was put in the hole—for protection from myself. As I sat in that PC cell, I tried to figure out a way to finish the job I had started, when I heard the man in the cell next to me singing. It was Sean. He was singing a poem he had written. The words and melody echoed through the walls:

> When I got down on my knees and prayed,
> this is what God had to say.
> Jesus will wash your sins away,
> if you'll just choose to live My way.
> From the dark of night till the dawn of day,
> Jesus will walk with you all the way.
> Share My love with mom and dad,
> share my love with all mankind,
> For my Son has died for all your sins,
> He gave His life so you may live.
> So if you'll stand by Me for evermore,
> My Son Jesus will let you through heaven's door!

"Here Sean was, facing execution, and he was in the next cell singing his heart out, praising the Lord. I'm facing ten years at most, and I was contemplating suicide. I needed some of what he had. Jesus!

"Jan, I could be used as a classic ad for a drug rehabilitation center. I had it all. I had my own real estate company, a big house, a pretty wife, three kids, two fancy cars, and a cocaine habit. First I lost the business, then the house, then my wife and children. I sold the cars and sniffed that money up my nose. The typical ad for cocaine abuse is, 'Would you die for me?' My answer was 'Yes, I'd die for you!' Jan, I lost everything dear to me and I still wanted more cocaine. I went out and robbed two banks to buy it.

"Sean showed me my life isn't ruined, just broken. Jesus is a carpenter. He'll restore it from the termite-eaten foundation to the leaky roof. I'll never forget Sean. He not only saved my life, he also saved my soul. Have you ever heard him sing 'Amazing Grace?'"

I grinned.

The other four men Sean led to the Lord called Gary and I from jail and asked questions Sean wasn't able to answer, but we never had an opportunity to meet with them because of our schedules. They each said the same thing—it was Sean's joy that made them decide to give Christ a chance.

The day of Sean's second trial, I was nervous as I walked into the courtroom. Sean's attorney asked me to go on the stand as Sean's chaplain and as a character witness. Sean had relieved me of any penitent privilege and said it was okay to share any part of his past or his childhood in the courtroom. As Sean stood before the three judges, the TV camera started to hum and the reporters from the *Las Vegas Review Journal* and the *Las Vegas Sun* picked up their pens.

"Your Honor," Sean began, "I know I asked for the death penalty and, in the first hearing, you granted me my wish. I was happy as I left the courtroom, but something happened that night as I sat on my bunk. I started wondering if I would go to heaven or hell when I was executed—and I didn't know. But since then I've become a Christian, and I can no longer ask you to take my life. I have to trust that God is now in control of my life. Anything I do is for the Lord and to glorify God. I'm sure you think I'm trying to make a mockery of this court, but I assure you I'm not. In fact I'm very embarrassed to stand here and tell you what is in my heart."

As Sean was seated, the judges called a recess and left the bench. Two guards escorted Sean to a small cell behind the courtroom. Within minutes they came back to the courtroom and asked me to follow them. They told me Sean was asking for me.

"Oh Mama, I was so nervous! Did you see my legs shaking? Do you think I did okay? Do you think I embarrassed God?"

I turned to the guard and said, "Can you open the cell door for me? He sure could use a hug!"

"Oh hell, why not?" one said to the other, "we've broken every rule anyway just having her back here." With that the guard opened up the cell door and allowed me to enter.

After we hugged, I asked Sean if he would like to have prayer with me. As he gave an approving nod, the guard whispered that I must hurry as the clerk would be coming at any moment. As we bowed our heads I said, "Thank you Lord for this situation and the glorious victory You will win because of it! Amen."

Moments later the court clerk came to the door and announced the judges were ready to return and that we had to enter the courtroom. I glanced at Sean and asked, "Are you okay now, little one?"

"I'm okay, Mama." Sean's smile confirmed his words.

As one of the guards escorted me back to the courtroom, he told me that both he and his partner were Christians and they would look after Sean.

The judge announced they would give Sean two weeks to prepare for a penalty hearing to determine his sentence. With that announcement the three judges left the courtroom, and the news media followed in one mass exodus!

As the evening news anchor for Channel 3 opened his news broadcast, he said, "An amazing new development has taken place in the trial of Sean Flanagan. As the second trial was to begin, Mr. Flanagan announced he had found God and had a change of heart. In the first trial he demanded the death penalty but now claims he wants to live!"

Two clips were flashed on the screen. The first showed Sean, with his head shaved during his first penalty hearing, laughing and joking with the prosecutor and playing up to the TV cameras. The second clip was of the day's hearing: Sean with his red hair cropping up, humbly telling the judges he was a new Christian. The show's co-host commented, "I can see where this sounds like a lot of phony baloney to our viewers. Maybe Flanagan is playing games with the court."

The newsman injected, "there was a definite change of attitude in that man today, you could see it in the courtroom. I tried to show it by playing both videos. He was laughing and joking two weeks ago—today he was a completely different person. Something amazing happened!"

On Wednesday, June 1, 1988, Sean appeared before the three judges for his second penalty hearing. I fidgeted nervously in my seat as I waited to be called to the stand. The prosecutor was one of the toughest in Nevada, and I knew he would do everything in his power to discredit me as a witness.

"Oh Lord," I whispered as I bowed my head, "Give me courage to speak up boldly on Sean's behalf. Just put the truth in my mouth and sit at my side as I am cross-examined by the prosecutor. Lord, you know because of the years I spent as an abused wife at the hands of my first husband—I crumble under intimidation. Give me the mettle to stand tall for You and Sean. Amen."

With head held high, I stepped into the witness box and raised my right hand and affirmed to tell the truth. I'm certain I looked calm, but I was trembling inside. Sean's attorney smiled as he stood at the defendant's table.

I knew he was trying to reassure me and keep me calm. "Mrs. Hoffman," he began, "would you tell the court how you came to know the defendant?" After I explained, he said, "Are there any special circumstances you'd like to tell the court that might help them understand Sean better?"

Because Sean gave me freedom to express the confidences he had shared with me, I told the judges everything—the physical abuse, the sexual abuse, the neglect of his natural mother, and the incest. I went on to say I thought a great deal of damage had been done emotionally to Sean because of these experiences as a child, and I asked the judges to consider that when they made their decisions.

When I finished, Sean's attorney sat down and the prosecutor stood up. "Oh oh, Lord," I silently prayed, "You promised You would never leave me or forsake me. Please be with me now."

"Mrs. Hoffman," the prosecutor said, "are you a psychologist or a psychiatrist?"

"No sir, I'm not."

"Well then, Mrs. Hoffman, you are not a qualified witness are you? What gives you the ability to determine Mr. Flanagan's mental state or the damage that may have been done?"

"Sir, my daughter was sexually abused from the age of three to the age of eleven. I lived the nightmare of trying to help her recover. I think personal experience gives me a great deal of credibility. I've seen firsthand the damage sexual and physical abuse does to a child!"

That seemed to rattle him a little, but he went on, "Well, I'm sorry about your daughter, but Mr. Flanagan has been manipulating this court since his arrest. What makes you think he isn't manipulating you right now?"

"Well sir, you sent a razor to Sean's cell this morning with a guard, and you asked the guard to tell Sean you thought he looked good with his head shaved. Weren't you trying to manipulate Sean?"

"I appreciate that comment," the prosecutor said, but I could tell by the black scowl on his face, he didn't appreciate it at all. I didn't care, it was the truth. With that I was curtly dismissed.

Within an hour the judges handed Sean his second death sentence.

"Mama, Dad, don't worry," Sean comforted Gary and me when we went to visit him that night, "God is in control." We were given an extra long visit with him that night. The visiting room guard was a Christian and told us to stay until visiting hour was over if we wanted to. Sean was in a surprisingly cheerful mood. He was transported to death row the next day.

Because of the damage done to Sean as a child, his emotional swings were radical. He read his Bible night and day, and Gary and I were amazed at his growth as a Christian. But Sean tended to be a legalist. He had difficulty with issues that could not be set down in black and white. The anxiety this caused him was illustrated by his inability to give up cigarettes, though he instantly gave up swearing and girlie magazines. He thought he would go to hell because he couldn't quit smoking. We assured him he wouldn't and encouraged him to pray about it.

"Sean, the apostle Paul prayed three times to have the thorn in his flesh removed. God told him 'no.' Where Paul was weak, He would be his strength. If we never admit to God that we are weak, we never give Him permission to be our strength! Quit trying to do it yourself and let Him help you."

Shortly after Sean was placed on death row, an inmate who constantly intimidated everyone was put in his cell block. All the inmates warned the guards they didn't want this man living with them, that he constantly caused trouble, but the guards put him in that cell block anyway.

A fight broke out and the inmate was injured. Sean "snitched" on everyone involved in the fight.

Because of that, he was placed in the lock-down unit for safekeeping. He was placed in the same cell block with the prison's toughest convicts. One day when the prison's most notorious convict was out on the tier, Sean called him over to his door. He started talking about Christ and this convict said, "Flanagan—I can tell right now—you and I aren't going to be real tight!"

Sean withdrew into a shell. His letters became few, although he continued to phone once a week. His despondence grew until one day he announced he was giving up his appeals rights and wanted to be executed. He had been listening to a Christian radio station and had ascertained from the preacher's teaching that he had to be executed to be forgiven.

After several months, the warden moved Sean back into the main death row unit, but to a different wing. Although he had freedom to go out on the tier with the other men, he was afraid because of the snitch label he was wearing. The Christians on the tier went to Sean's cell and told him he wouldn't have problems with anyone and encouraged him to join them for Bible studies and fellowship. Sean had the guard unlock his door.

Sean's depression didn't lift as I had hoped it would when he was placed with this Christian group of men. Instead it seemed to intensify. He not only insisted that he had to be executed, he was convinced he was the only Christian on Nevada's death row.

On one occasion when Sean received a small order he had placed with the prison's store, he was mistakenly given a five dollar book of stamps. He could have kept them, but he gave them back. It doesn't seem like a very big deal, but stamps are as good as money in prison and Sean had very little money to buy everyday necessities. The guard couldn't believe it when Sean handed them back. His honesty was a witness to that guard and to Jeff Farmer, who witnessed the incident.

These men rallied around Sean, sharing Scripture with him. They spent hours each day trying to show Sean that with His death on the cross Jesus paid the full price for all sin. Sean's spilled blood would not mingle with Christ's to aide in God's forgiveness of Sean.

Sean continued to listen to the radio broadcasts and informed his attorney he wanted the courts to set his execution date. He confined himself to his cell and refused to come out except for the few phone calls he made. After he contacted his attorney to make known his decision, Sean called Gary and me to tell us. After he told us his intentions I said, "Oh honey, are you sure this is what you want?"

"Oh yes, Mama, I'm sure. I just want to go home to be with Jesus!"

On June 23, 1989, four days after Bud Thompson was executed, Sean was escorted into the execution chamber by five correctional officers. Intravenous tubes were placed in each of his arms and he was given a lethal dose of three drugs. As the drugs began to flow, Sean looked at his prosecuting attorney, and with his last breath said, "You are a just man—I love you."

As the prosecutor stood before the news media after the execution, he commented that Sean died believing he was atoning his sins, but he remained unconvinced God could forgive such a brutal killer.

When Bud Thompson was executed, a reporter contacted me and I consented to give an interview. The first question I was asked was whether or not I thought Bud was committing state-sanctioned suicide because he had given up his appeals rights, and how I thought God felt about it. I responded with a question, "If you learned you had terminal cancer and there was a slight chance cobalt treatment and chemotherapy would cure you, would it be suicide if you refused the painful treatment?"

"Mrs. Hoffman," he continued, "How do you feel about voluntary executions?"

"What does it gain society to execute a person who wants to die? Where is the retribution? Where is the deterrent value? Where is the gratification to the victim's family? Retribution rarely satisfies because it is never enough."

The day after Sean was executed, Gary was contacted by a reporter from Channel 3 TV and asked to give an interview. When asked what he thought of Sean's voluntary execution, Gary replied, "Jan and I don't sit in judgment of anyone, that's God's job. Every time we went to see Sean, he bubbled over with enthusiasm. He had either written a new poem or found a new verse of Scripture he wanted to share. He was always happy and smiling. That's how I want to remember him. We did what God called us to do—we loved him. We love them all!"

CHAPTER NINE
Roses Have Thorns

"Keep on loving each other as brothers. Do not forget to entertain strangers, for by so doing some people have entertained angels without knowing it. Remember those in prison as if you were their fellow prisoners, and those who are mistreated as if you yourselves were suffering."

Hebrews 13:1-3

I constantly struggle with myself, wondering why I do what I do. The letters we receive are so inspiring and uplifting I ask, "Am I doing this for you, Lord, or am I doing it because the strokes feel so good? Does anyone else in ministry ever have this same struggle, Father?"

God showed me the good strokes the ministry receives are hugs from Him, to tide us through the bad times which are sure to come because where there are roses, there are sure to be thorns. For example, we received this letter from a prisoner:

> *You think all those guys who write for The Rising Son are such hot shot Christians. Well you printed an article from a jerk here, and he's no more a Christian than I am. When you print those articles, how do you know if they are really Christians or playing you for suckers?*

I wrote back and said, "You're absolutely right, I don't know if all the people who submit articles for *The Rising Son* are Christians or if they are running a con. I can't be

there to look over everyone's shoulders. I figure it this
way, if a person's article brings glory to God, I'll print it.
At least for the few hours he spent writing that article, his
mind is on God. Maybe, just maybe, the seeds he is
attempting to plant in someone else's heart will take root
and grow in his own. How do I know if the person sitting
next to me in church on Sunday is really a Christian? I
don't, but it's not my job to judge. I'll leave that to God,
because only He knows what is in the heart."

A non-Christian prisoner who we corresponded with
for several years once asked, "How can you and Gary be so
open and honest? Aren't you afraid people will trample all
over your backs?"

After giving his question careful consideration, I
responded, "No, we're not afraid because, you see, the
worst thing that will happen if people trample on our
backs is that they will get love all over their feet."

We've been conned, scammed, and flim-flammed by
the best of them. One man wrote and asked us for five
hundred dollars for an attorney. He used every technique
known to man in that one letter. He pleaded, begged, and
put us on a guilt trip by saying, "If you don't pay the
electric bill for one month, you can always have it turned
on again next month, but if I am executed, my life can't be
turned back on again." We checked with some attorneys
to see where he was in the appeals process, and we learned
he was not in as imminent danger of execution as he had
indicated.

We know we don't have a choir boy ministry. This we
do know, Jesus died for the cons, murderers, scammers,
and the flim-flammers the same way He died for Gary and
me. They just don't know it yet! That's our job—to tell
them. The Bible promises, "Therefore, if anyone is in
Christ, he is a new creation; the old has gone, and the new
has come!" (2 Corinthians 5:17).

We have also received letters from people who were angered by our newsletter and ministry in general. The following two letters were particularly disturbing to read because we could feel the heartache and bitterness that promoted them.

Gary and Janalee,

As a parent of a young child who was criminally raped and brutally mutilated, I cannot understand both your thinking of coddling murderers on death row.

I think you both should spend your time with families of the victims in strengthening their souls to God to carry on in life.

Maybe some in death row are in there for only one crime in their life but reading your booklet, The Rising Son, not one shows any remorse for the crime!

Ted Bundy killed over sixty young women. Never showed remorse.

Charles Manson, in his religious cult, trained young girls that killing was justified. One of his students ripped open the stomach of pregnant Sharon Tate and mutilated the fetus.

John Hinckley attempted to assassinate the President of the United States and also terrorized movie star Jodi Foster for years through phone calls and mail. He also wrote letters to Manson.

All your criminals who write letters to The Rising Son say they "found Jesus." I found a dead body—my child!

God said, "Thou shalt not kill" and also said "an eye for an eye" if you do.

As a pleading parent, I beg you to console the victim's families, not killers.

Janalee and Gary,

I was given a copy of your booklet The Rising Son by a friend of mine, to read and return with a response to the death penalty. In my opinion it is not a penalty but it is a justice according to the law of the land.

Any person who willfully snuffs out the life of a victim is robbing him of the right to live. Killing the person also kills his family.

All of your death row writers talk of returning to God and God will forgive them upon execution. Please, I don't want to meet criminals in heaven when it's my turn to die. How can I be sure they are rehabilitated?

None of these writers show remorse for their victims or their families. They all claim bad upbringing and child abuse.

My childhood was abuse and bad environment but I pulled through and led a clean, lawful life.

Most of your death row people are there for as long as ten years. The families of the victims will spend eternity in sorrow. Is this fair?

Your group would do the world a favor if you spend time consoling and helping the family of murdered sons or husbands.

When judgement day arrives what will you tell St. Peter? I wish I was there to hear your answer. Save the good people, not the scum.

I did not answer these letters when I received them, but I would like to answer them now.

Dear friends,

Gary and I feel your sorrow, pain, and loss, and although I realize it is of little consolation, our hearts go out to you. We want you to know that in spite of our ministry to people on death row, we do have a heart for the victims and their families. My own daughter was a victim of sexual abuse from the age of three to eleven without my knowledge at that time, and I was a battered wife. Today I know the bitterness, anger, and, vengeance a victim feels.

By God's good grace, my precious daughter is whole now and so am I. Gary's understanding and patience did much to aid the healing process for both of us. When I was filled with hostility, he showed me that kind of hatred would destroy me.

Gary sat me down one night and read the parable of "The Unmerciful Servant" in Matthew 18:21. After he read it, I began to realize how much God had forgiven me, and I must also be forgiving of the man who had stolen my daughter's innocence. God had long ago restored my self esteem, which the abuse had robbed me of, but I was bitter and angry over what this man had done to my innocent little daughter.

I had taken on God's job in judging him. The Lord called me to pray for my adversary. I learned it is difficult to have a clenched fist when your hands are together in prayer. Although it was not easy at first, gradually I began to sincerely ask God to heal him emotionally and spiritually. I spent seven years praying for the man who had molested my daughter before God finally set me free.

Gary and I work with victim's support groups and, in fact, as a result of The Rising Son, one young woman went to the county jail to confront the man who had murdered her sister and she presented the Gospel to him. She told him that it was only because of God's love that she was able to visit him, and that God's love allowed her to love and forgive him.

When Nancy shared this with members of her group, they were angry at her. Nancy told them, "I've been attending these meetings for months and all we do is continue to relive the crimes, in detail, over and over again. We keep feeding on the misery and pain of our loss. It's about time we started to heal. We have all had loved ones ripped away from us, but to my way of thinking, heaven isn't such a bad deal for them."

Bill Pelke is another example of how God can heal a victim's family through a forgiving heart. Bill's grandmother, who was a Sunday School teacher, was murdered. A group of high school girls tricked her into letting them in her house by telling her they wanted to learn about the Bible. These girls were high on marijuana and wine and their real motive was to rob her. Bill's grandmother was stabbed thirty three times. A fifteen-year-old-girl named Paula was sentenced to death for this crime.

Bill was filled with bitterness. He had been especially close to his grandmother. One night while Bill was alone at work, God pressed upon his heart to forgive Paula. Over his family's objection, Bill wrote to her and told her that he had forgiven her and was praying for her. Because of his ministering to Paula, she has repented of her sins and she has made her peace with God.

Bill now heads one of the largest victim's groups in Indiana, Murder Victim's Families for Reconciliation. He places an emphasis on healing through forgiveness.

Bill just received a letter from a death row prisoner in the men's unit who will soon be receiving an execution date. In his letter he said, "My soul hurts and I never told the victim's mother how sorry I am." This man was in a half-way house at the time of the crime and, although he was not a suspect, came forward and confessed. His jury recommended a life sentence, but the judge sentenced him to death. He asked Bill to pray for him and help him make his peace with God. I have no doubt that

Bill will be a beacon shining in the darkness to lead this lost soul to Christ.

Although Gary and I are deeply sensitive toward the victims and their families, God didn't call us to a victim ministry, He called us to a prison ministry. Jesus must have had a special place in His own heart for people in prison, because He commanded us to visit them in Matthew 25:31-46.

There is the possibility that some of the prisoners are conning us, with Christian sounding words, but the fact is, they can't con God, for "nothing in all creation is hidden from God's sight. Everything is uncovered and laid bare before the eyes of Him to whom we must give account" (Hebrews 4:13).

He is the righteous judge, and looks deep inside the heart where our eyes cannot see. While some may not be sincere, we are convinced that many have had a born again experience, because we see the good fruit that they continue to produce.

Our priority is this: If we can just save one soul from an eternity in hell, than we know that what we are doing is important to God, because the Bible says "...your Father in heaven is not willing that any of these little ones should be lost" (Matthew 18:14).

You are right when you said that many of the prisoners talk about the abuse they suffered as children and while we agree that many people who were abused as children grow up to be whole and healthy adults, some don't. According to the national foundation called, Child Help U.S.A., over 90 percent of the prisoners on death row were abused as children.

Eddie Cole was a perfect example. In the last interview he gave before his execution, he stressed the dangers of child abuse with these words:

"In a parting shot I will say, take two children. One has the aid of family and friends who are aware of

the abuse and help the child; the family or friends of the
other child know of the harsh treatment, but do nothing
about it! Which child is most likely to turn out bad?
Maybe neither, but my bet would go on the child without
help.

"Those parents who abuse their children should be
made to understand, that in some cases they are putting
something in motion that they may in time come to regret.
If they would only realize what they are doing, they
wouldn't do it. Prevention is the answer, and it begins in
childhood."

Over the years as we have become friends with
these prisoners on death row, and as their trust in us has
grown, many have shared their childhood stories, and we
have come to feel that in a sense ours is a victim ministry.
We are ministering to adults who were abused as children
and grew up to abuse others.

Child abuse does untold damage and our society
must be vigilant about this new generation of children.
There is a segment of our society that is made up of
damaged people and they are reproducing themselves. I do
not mean to offer child abuse as an excuse for murder.
Murder is a horrible crime, but rather I offer it as an
explanation of how lives can become so out of control.

The Rising Son does not address the issue of
capital punishment. Since we believe that Jesus died for
all sin, and has the ability to create in us a new spirit, its
purpose is to help these prisoners make their peace with
God before they go to stand before Him. Remember "...if
Christ is in you, your body is dead because of sin, yet your
spirit is alive because of righteousness" (Romans 8:10).

We have been advised by attorneys not to print
anything that could hurt a prisoner's appeal which might
be pending in court, so for that reason, we omit anything
from their articles that could be detrimental, such as their
great remorse. We apologize to you and to them for this,

but we must follow a set of guidelines when we are editing.

     Because the majority of our newsletters are sent to prisoners on death row, we select articles which will minister to them—testimonies of God's power, peace, and grace working in the author's own life.

     We are sorry for the loss of your loved ones and we pray that the Lord will comfort you and fill your hearts with peace to sustain you until you join them in heaven. Rather than reliving the pain of the past, I urge you to look forward to the glorious day when you shall be together again, in a place where every tear will be wiped from your eyes and where there will be no more death, or mourning or crying or pain.

     May God put a rainbow in your heart for now, to sustain you until then.

          Sincerely,
          Janalee Hoffman

When people accept Jesus into their hearts and repent of their sins, this act opens a door for an interaction to take place between them and God, because they become His children. It can also change their behavior toward others around them. Those who have not repented do not share this same liberty with God.

As an example: you would more than likely be offended if a neighbor child walked into your house and said, "My birthday is next Monday, here is a list of the things I want." On the other hand, if your child came to you and said, "there are several things I would like for my birthday, so I made out a list," you would probably be happy to look over this list to see what your budget would allow you to buy. After all, this is your child and that special relationship entitles him or her to privileges that the neighbor child doesn't share.

As parents, we not only want our children to have "the good life," but we are also concerned for the condition of their hearts. So it is with our heavenly father. God doesn't want His children to harbor bitterness, hatred, anger, or vengeance in their hearts. He wants His children to be loving toward each other, and to be filled with peace, contentment, and joy. He wants them to be forgiving of each other and to ask for forgiveness if they have done something to hurt another person.

As an invited guest in Christians' hearts, Jesus goes from room to room and carefully cleans His new homes. The benefit society receives from a prisoner "getting right with God," is that Jesus may inspire him or her to contact the victim or the victim's family and express remorse and try to make amends. This can set the victim free from the bondage of bitterness and allow the healing process to begin. Once healing starts, people are free to get on with their lives.

Although it may be the desire of their hearts, expressing remorse is more difficult in the case of prisoners who are on death row. Their attorneys discourage this, as it can impair the appeals process.

For instance, in the case of a death row prisoner named David, he has repented and made his peace with God, but now he feels a compelling need to let his victim's family know how sorry he is for his crime. His goal is not to seek a reduction in his sentence, but rather, to promote healing in the hearts of the family members he hurt. Whether they forgive him or not, he feels he must show them his deep remorse.

David's lawyer does not want him to contact the family because of fear it will negatively affect his appeal, which is pending in court. In a recent letter, David told us that he has more faith in the "Righteous Judge" than the judicial system. He has such strong convictions that he is contemplating ignoring the objections of his attorney and writing the letter anyway.

In another case, a young prisoner named Richard became a Christian while he waited in county jail to go to trial for a burglary and rape charge. After several months, Richard learned that another man was convicted of first degree murder for a crime he himself had committed, but was never charged with. Richard came forward, over the protest of his attorney, family, and friends, and confessed to the crime. The other man was set free. Richard was then charged with murder, tried, and sentenced to death. He has since contacted both the rape victim and the family of the woman he murdered and has expressed his remorse.

The woman he raped has forgiven him. He has peace, knowing she is healing from the emotional wounds he inflicted upon her. It was her generous forgiveness that has promoted this healing in her own heart. Richard has not heard from the family of the woman he murdered. He continues to pray for this family.

We do not interfere with the appeals process but we do urge the prisoners to pray for the victims and their families, and then to write or contact them after they have exhausted all of their appeals.

The point is, there are many healing processes that take place from a change in heart and attitude. Often times, this healing does not just occur for the person who has accepted Christ, but for others who surround that person—the family, friends, and the family and friends of people that person has harmed. It is conceivable that many people will change and grow from the exposure of the truth—good or bad—for the Bible says, "the truth will set you free" (John 8:32).

The anonymous poem on the next page is for all to consider:

NO ONE EXPECTED ME

I dreamed death came the other night;
　And heaven's gates swung wide.
With kindly grace an angel
　Ushered me inside.

And there, to my astonishment,
　Stood folks I'd known on earth.
Some I'd judged and labeled
　Unfit or of little worth.

Indignant words rose to my lips,
　But never were set free;
For every face showed stunned surprise,
　No one expected me!

After a particularly difficult day, Henry called us and said, "Jan, it's a lot of hard work working for Jesus." The simplicity and innocence of that statement has helped me smile my way through many difficult situations which the ministry has been confronted with.

Gary and I ask ourselves one question in all situations, good or bad, "What would Jesus do?" This is not always an easy question to answer. One thing is certain, Jesus wouldn't quit, nor will we, even though at times we feel like giving up. We will continue on as the apostle Paul mandated in Ephesians 2:10, "For we are God's workmanship, created in Christ Jesus to do good works, which God prepared in advance for us to do."

EPILOGUE

OLD MAN DOING TIME

He couldn't read or write much, he barely knew his age;
As worthless as an old book, missing every other page.
No one went to see him, or cared to send a dime;
His family had all turned their back, on the old man doin' time!

His clothes in need of washing, his face in need of shave;   His
heart in need of someone, before he found his grave.
His life had been a sad one, unlike yours or mine;
For no one cared about, the old man doin' time!

His hands that held his Bible, the book he called his friend;   Were
tarnished from the Buglar stains, "a free tobacco blend."
And with silver hair atop, a face with aging lines;
There was a heart as big as Texas, in the old man doin' time.

Then one morn at twilight, some visitors came to be;
The angels took the old man, and finally set him free.
So now he's up there somewhere, he's found his peace of mind.
Now everybody's missing the old man doin' time!

by Byron Ashley Parker, death row, Jackson, Georgia

Gary and I find it difficult to believe this ministry is entering its eighth year. It's been a time of joy, inspiration, fulfillment, and excitement as we have watched the power of God unleashed in our nation's death rows.

The Lord in His wisdom even allows Gary and I to indulge in laughter on occasion. One day of sunshine can wipe out a year of rain. The Bible says in Ecclesiastes 3:4 that there is a time for everything, "a time to weep and a time to laugh."

Recently, a death row prisoner sent us a computerized sweepstakes letter he had received from a magazine clearing house. It read:

Dear Mr. Brooks:

You'll be able to buy a new home in the best part of Angola...drive down death row in a brand new car every year...leave Louisiana for an exotic around-the-world vacation, and much more.

This prisoner has a delightful sense of humor and was as amused by this letter as we were. Gary and I are certain, because of his circumstances, the idea of a vacation in an exotic place is more appealing than impressing his neighbors by driving a new car up and down death row.

After years of corresponding with the prisoners, our reward is to be able to go to their prison and visit with them. I was able to return to Nashville and see Steve West and Gerald Laney for a second time in 1989.

They have been moved from the century-old prison where they were incarcerated on my first visit to a new facility several miles away. Even though the new prison looks like a college campus rather than a monstrous castle-like fortress, the visiting conditions were better in the old prison. While visiting with Steve and Gerald, I was able to meet and visit with sixteen other men from their death row unit.

In the past year, Steve's wife has asked him for a divorce and has given their three daughters up for adoption. Steve was so in love with his wife and girls that his heart was broken and his faith was bitterly tested. He experienced a deep depression and we feared that he would walk away from the Lord, but he held on to the hem of Jesus' robe and he continues to serve God. Now his faith is stronger than ever.

Gerald's book is almost complete and ready to submit to a publisher. His story depicts a child with an unrecognized learning disability that grew into an outlaw motorcycle gang member. I could feel the love of Christ working in his heart as I read his manuscript and I was awed by the power of God to change even the most despicable person's life. His near-death experience and seeing the flames of hell as he hurled towards them will keep his readers on the edge of their seats. One chapter I found particularly moving was when Gerald saved a guard's life, at the risk of losing his own, during a prison riot.

Both Steve and Gerald are awaiting the outcome of their appeals.

In the fall of 1989, the men on Nevada's death row were transferred to a new prison. Henry Dawson continues to hold Bible studies every day and, in addition, the prison now has a chaplain. The chaplain comes into the death row unit every Wednesday and holds Bible studies. Last week, twenty-one of the men attended. He will soon baptize eight of them.

After fifteen years, Pete Deutscher's appeal was heard and his attorney informed him that his sentence had been overturned. Pete is waiting while the prosecutor appeals the decision of the high court, but he may get a new trial.

Gregory Collier went into such deep depression that he committed suicide. He was found in his cell by a guard, during a routine count of the men. He strangled himself with an electrical cord. Gregory was twenty-eight years old.

Since our ministry began, four men have been executed on Nevada's death row. Carroll Edward Cole, Bud Thompson, Sean Flanagan, and Thomas Ball have all gone home to be with the Lord. The other men are still waiting for the outcome of their appeals.

We never received the cassette tape Bud and Sean promised. They were so excited when the warden promised them the use of a tape recorder for their final good-byes. Sean said, "Mama, I'll sing 'Amazing Grace' for you and when you play it, I want you to remember how happy we were the night we sang it together at the jail."

Gary and I feel certain they each made us a tape or, at least, wrote a letter; because it took six months to receive Eddie's good-bye letter, we patiently waited to hear from Sean and Bud. Did they get misplaced? Were they lost in the mail? Did they decide not to say good-bye? We don't know what happened, but we never heard from either one of them.

We have not visited with the men since they have been in the new prison, but we are looking forward to making the trip soon.

In June, 1990, while attending a chaplains' conference in Indianapolis, Indiana, I was able to visit the women's death row unit, where I visited with Paula and Lois. Since that visit, each of their death sentences has been overturned to sixty-year sentences.

Paula has no children, but Lois has three. They resided at the Indiana Soldiers and Sailors Children home for years, but are now living with their elderly grandmother. Lois rarely sees her children because her mother isn't able to afford the trip often. We are seeking a sponsor or church to help transport them to the prison.

On October 1, 1991, an attorney for Frank Rodriguez asked me if I would come to Colorado. During his investigation on Frank's behalf, he discovered that Frank had been severely abused as a child by his father. In

addition to the physical abuse, he suspected that Frank
had also been sexually molested. While Frank would
discuss the physical abuse, he refused to acknowledge the
sexual abuse his attorney had discovered.

During a phone conversation with Frank, he
tentatively discussed the sexual abuse with Gary and me.
He said, "My attorney wants me to talk about it, but he
doesn't have to live in this prison. If the other men find
out, do you know what they will do to me? In all these
years I haven't told anyone what happened. I just blocked
it out of my mind and forgot about it. I'm ashamed of
what my father did to me and I just want to forget about it.
It's too painful to remember. Mother and Dad, what
should I do?"

Gary and I both advised him to be opened and honest
with his attorney. I said, "Look, Frank, you have trusted
God with every other area of your life, why not trust him
with this? For your own sake, it's time you talked about
what happened to you. You can push it out of your mind,
but those old wounds are still there. If you had a bullet in
your leg and you put a bandage over it, no one would
know it was there, but it would fester and poison your
whole system. The bullet needs to be removed before
healing can take place. After it is removed and the wound
heals, it will leave a scar, but your life can go on. That's
the way it is with an emotional wound. My daughter was
sexually molested and it was only after she began talking
about what happened that her healing began."

Frank said, "Mother, I think if my attorney brought you
to the prison with him, I might be able to talk about it. I
believe you can help me overcome my embarrassment. If
he can arrange for you to come, will you help me?"

Gary jumped in and said, "Frank, she'll be there. Have
your attorney contact us with the arrangements."

Two weeks later I was on my way to Denver. Frank's
attorney picked me up at the airport and we drove to

Canon City, where the prison is located. There are three men on Colorado's death row. While we were at the prison, the attorney arranged for me to visit with each of them.

Seeing Gary Davis for the first time was a special blessing. Gary had led Frank to the Lord through a quarter-sized hole between their cells. I was surprised at how bashful he was, especially after several years of correspondence with each other. A few days after I returned home I received a letter from Gary. He wrote, "That is the first contact visit I have had in five years and the first hug."

The first morning of our three-day visit with Frank was spent in relaxed conversation. On the drive to the prison, I mentioned to his attorney that I didn't want Frank to think he was being pounced on and that I would like to start off with a carefree and enjoyable visit. He agreed and said this was his plan as well.

When we returned to the prison after lunch, I gave Frank a letter that my daughter had written to him. She thought it might help him if she shared a little of her own experience.

October 15, 1991

Dear Frank,

I hope you don't mind my writing but Mom talks about you so often, I feel like we're family. I don't know if Mom has mentioned me, so please allow me to introduce myself. My name is Ann and I have four children. Jessa is eleven, Christopher is seven, Kyle is five, and Janalee is two. Needless to say, my hands are full. I'm thirty-one years old and like yourself, I take it one day at a time.

I know our mom is probably there with you now, sharing this letter. This is as I wanted it to be. Frank, she is absolutely trustworthy. I know you are in your hour of need, and I want you to know when I was in my hour of need, which was more often than I'd like to admit, Mom was always there. All 98 percent water and 100 percent love.

Believe me when I tell you that you cannot offend or embarrass her. She has never judged nor criticized, only offered her much-needed support. Without her I could never have achieved mental health. Now I'm the first to admit I have a lot of work to do in that department. But by the good grace of God, I'm on my way.

My sense of well-being and the healing process started only after I opened up and began to unload all that extra baggage. I didn't want to talk about what happened to me, but once it was out in the open, I began to realize that I had nothing to be ashamed of. The shame that I had hidden in the cracks of my heart for years wasn't even mine.

Very much like yourself, I was victimized by a bastard father who's love was never to be mine. How devastating it was to grow up used and abused—longing to be loved! Again, like yourself, my father decided physical and mental abuse wasn't enough torture to inflict on his trusting child. At the age of six he began to sexually abuse me. He found gratification in humiliating my innocent child's body.

He let me know I was disgusting to him because I would someday grow into a woman. By my teens, he had planted a seed in my head that took me fifteen years to uproot. My father introduced me to drugs while I was a young teenager and I became a drug addict. By the age of eighteen I had become a prostitute. I believed that my life's purpose was to give men pleasure. I had no sense of self worth.

Now I'm sure you must wonder what roll my mother played in all of this. Let me explain. She was

little more than a child herself when I was born, she was
only seventeen. We grew up together.

She was as much a victim as I was. Even as a
little girl I knew if I were to say anything about what my
father was doing to me, that harm would come to her.
My child's mind could not handle that. I couldn't let my
only friend be beaten because of me. The role she played
later was to guide me to become the Christian woman I
am today and help me heal mentally and emotionally.
Mental health is a legacy I can now pass onto my children.

There is so much I want to share and if our
friendship grows, I'm sure we can do just that. But right
now I think it's important to tell you how my story ends.
The healing process isn't easy Frank, and to say it is would
be a lie. Fifteen years of hell cannot be forgotten in one
day or even one year. It is something we will deal with
for the rest of our lives. But the healing must start
somewhere.

"When" and "how" the healing first started for me
is hard to say. So I can only tell you where I am now.
Frank, we are the victims. We never asked for that which
was given to us. I was a thief, a whore, and a drug
peddler. All the time lying to myself about it. This
lifestyle was a cover to hide the damaged child that lived
inside of me. I had a hole in my soul that only Jesus could
fill—even though I didn't realize it at the time.

I can't change the things I was, so now I use
them to my advantage. I live in a trailer park which is a
hair from poverty level. I draw upon my past experiences
to counsel and to tough-love my neighbors. You can do the
same where you are, brother. Don't be afraid of what
others will think. Your peers may want you to believe
they had a fairy-tale life, but I assure you that they are
lying to you and to themselves. At least 50 percent of the
prisoners you look at today will have slept in the same bed

as you and 1 did. They just won't admit it. It takes
courage to tell it like it is.

I've seen the dark side of life, but now I'm living
in the light. As 1 look back, 1 realize all of these
experiences have made me who 1 am today. The bad has
made me strong and the good has kept me sweet.

My life is like an open book, but some pages are
more difficult to turn than others. Some people are
uncomfortable with my story, so 1 only share it when 1
know it will help others. For those who don't want to
face the harsh realities of what can and does happen to
children, they can read a Mother Goose nursery rhyme.

As a little girl, 1 had a dad who didn't deserve
my love, but 1 also had a heavenly Father who helped me
survive those years. Now, God has blessed me with a new
father who does deserve my love. Mom and Gary have
such big, loving hearts that God has decided there is
enough room in their hearts for you as well.

We can move mountains Frank, but we must focus
our eyes on the task before us and keep shoveling. Before
you know it, it will all be behind you and your life can
move forward. Because of times like these 1 went out and
bought myself a large economy-size shovel and 1 want you
to know, I'm right here beside you. Love you Frank.
Welcome to our family.

> *Your Sister,*
> *Ann*

Frank was so touched by Ann's letter that the flood
gates of his heart opened up and all the poison that his
abusive father put there came pouring out. He began with
the physical abuse, and detailed the times he was stripped
and made to stand in the bathtub while his father beat him
with an electrical appliance cord. The beatings were done

in the tub to prevent blood from staining anything in the house.

When Frank began to talk about the sexual abuse, both his attorney and I were surprised to learn that Frank had been sexually abused by two other family members, in addition to his father.

In the end, he said he no longer cared what the other men thought. He decided to write an article for *The Rising Son* and he asked me to print his name.

He turned to his attorney and said, "Mike, I know I will never get out of prison, but if I ever come out from under the sentence of death, I want to spend the rest of my life trying to reach the new kids who walk in these prison gates. If I can help them heal from the abuse they suffered and they can get their lives together so they will lead productive lives once they are out of prison—then my time in prison will have meaning."

Frank's and Gary's appeals are still pending in the courts. Chaplain Ben continues to visit them once a week for Bible studies and again for Sunday service.

Frank and I prayed that God would either change the heart of the guard who tormented him, or move him to a different shift. The guard was transferred to a different prison.

On November 16, 1991, I was invited by the men on Kentucky's death row to be a guest speaker at a banquet their warden allowed them to hold in the visiting room. While there I was introduced to twenty-one of the men.

The warden allowed this banquet to take place under the conditions that the men paid for the food and that each man invited only two guests. The men pooled their own money and with the assistance of several ministries were able to pay for the food.

When I was initially asked to be their guest, I told them that I didn't think I could afford the plane fare. They provided the funds for my trip, with the help of other ministries.

To our knowledge, this is the only prison in the country that permits their death row prisoners to attend chapel services. While they are in the chapel they are allowed to mix freely with the men from the yard, but they are required to wear red clothing. I was allowed to do the Sunday morning service.

The circulation for *The Rising Son* has now grown to over six thousand. It is mailed into 152 prisons, all fifty states, and thirty foreign countries. It now requires over twelve cases of paper to publish each issue. Because of the magnitude of the task, we now hire a professional printing company to print, collate, and staple the newsletter, although we continue to edit, type, and do the art layout. We no longer publish bi-monthly, but rather, we publish as often as our finances permit.

As our ministry has grown, we have developed several new areas of ministry in addition to *The Rising Son*. We have joined with Chuck Colson's Prison Fellowship and have sponsored over five hundred children for Project Angel Tree.

A publishing house supplies us with Christian books and cassette tapes which we mail to individual prisoners as well as to chaplains for their chapel library.

We have continued to develop our pen-friend ministry and there are currently over three hundred people ministering to prisoners on death row through letters. We consider this one of the most important aspects of our ministry.

Our greatest joy is witnessing how God is using these condemned prisoners to reach each other for His kingdom. These men and women are truly blooming where they are planted.

As I think of those we serve, I am reminded of a story Dr. Lloyd John Ogilvie tells in his book *The Beauty of Sharing*:

SHARING THE IMPOSSIBILITY OF IMPOSSIBILITIES

"For with God nothing will be impossible."

Luke 1:37

"I thank God there is a way out through Jesus Christ our Lord."

Romans 7:25

> There is a famous painting in which the artist depicts the great encounter between Faust and Satan. Faust gambled for his soul. The painting pictures the two sitting at a chessboard, the devil leering because he has checkmated Faust's king and knight. One day a famous master of chess went to the gallery in London to study the picture. He spent hours meditating on the seemingly impossible situation it depicted. He paced back and forth. Then, to the utter amazement of the other art viewers in the gallery, he shouted his discovery. "It's a lie!" he blurted. "It's a lie! The king and the knight have another move!"
>
> There's always another move for God. However black and grim things seem, He has a next move we could never have imagined. Whenever we are tempted to say, "I'm done in, I'm beaten, there's no hope left," the Lord is ready for His big move.
>
> Once we've experienced God's way out when we've found ourselves in a cul-de-sac of impossibility, we become people who can go to people who are worried and boxed in and say, "Be sure of this: God always has one more move!"

One of the condemned criminals hanging on the cross turned to Jesus and asked for an eleventh-hour reprieve. He said, "Jesus, remember me when you come into your kingdom." Jesus continues to promise paradise to those on death row who turn to Him—and His grace will lead them home. Yes, Dr. Ogilvie, "God always has one more move."

Photo © by Bernhard Williams Photography

About the Author

Janalee Hoffman, pictured here with her husband Gary, started her prison ministry with him almost ten years ago. The fruit of their labor is a blessing from the Lord called the Rising Son Ministry, which, over the years, has ministered to thousands of men and women in prison and on death row. Through a newsletter called *The Rising Son*, which is authored by the Christian men and women on death row, together Jan and Gary have reached hearts because of the grace of God.

The couple live in Las Vegas, Nevada, and they each have four children, and between them, fourteen grandchildren. They have also adopted countless children, brothers, and sisters in Christ through their years of ministry.

"Then the King will say to those on His right, 'Come, you who are blessed by my Father; take your inheritance, the kingdom prepared for you since the creation of the world. For I was hungry and you gave me something to eat, I was thirsty and you gave me something to drink, I was a stranger and you invited me in, I needed clothes and you clothed me, I was sick and you looked after me, I was in prison and you came to visit me.'"

Matthew 25:34-36

Although you may never hear the clanging of a steel-barred door closing behind you as you enter a prison, if you feel the Lord speaking to your heart, we would like to invite you to be our partner in this ministry. You can be an ambassador for the Lord and minister to those in prison without leaving the comfort of your home. It is the goal of this ministry to place a copy of this book in the hands of every person on death row. For those who already know the Lord, the book will encourage them. For those who don't, it may plant a seed in their hearts.

✂✃✂

1. I'll send a copy of your book to a prisoner   _____

2. I'll be a pen-friend to a prisoner   _____

3. I'll send a one-time donation in the amount of $ _____

4. I'll send a monthly donation in the amount of $ _____

5. I'll pray for your ministry   _____

6. Please send me a sample copy of *The Rising Son*   _____

Name:_____

Address:_____

City, State, Zip:_____

We are a nonprofit organization. All donations are tax deductible. We welcome speaking engagements and interviews. You can contact us by writing or calling:

Rising Son Ministry, Inc.
Attn: Gary and Janalee Hoffman
1829 E. Charleston, #100
Las Vegas, Nevada 89104